Second Edition

# Now Hear This!

## High Beginning
## Listening, Speaking & Pronunciation

# Barbara H. Foley

### Institute for Intensive English
### Union County College, New Jersey

Heinle & Heinle Publishers
A Division of Wadsworth, Inc.
Boston, MA 02116 U.S.A.

The publication of *Now Hear This, High Beginning Listening, Speaking, and Pronunciation, Second Edition,* was directed by the members of the Newbury House Publishing Team at Heinle & Heinle:

Erik Gundersen, Editorial Director
Gabrielle B. McDonald, Production Editor

Also participating in the publication of this program were:

Publisher: Stanley J. Galek
Editorial Production Manager: Elizabeth Holthaus
Managing Developmental Editor: Beth Kramer
Project Manager: Anita L. Raducanu/A+ Publishing Services
Assistant Editor: Karen P. Hazar
Associate Marketing Manager: Donna Hamilton
Production Assistant: Maryellen Eschmann
Manufacturing Coordinator: Mary Beth Lynch
Photo Coordinator: Martha Leibs-Heckly
Illustrator: Marcy Ramsey
Interior Designer: Sue Gerould/Perspectives
Cover Designer: Petra Hausberger

**PHOTO CREDITS**

Heinle & Heinle Publishers is a division of Wadsworth, Inc.

Manufactured in the United States of America

**Library of Congress Cataloging in Publication Data**

Foley, Barbara H.
    Now hear this! : high beginning listening, speaking &
    pronunciation / Barbara H. Foley.--2nd ed.
        p.    cm.
    1. English language--Textbooks for foreign speakers.  2. English
    language--Pronunciation by foreign speakers.  3. English language-
    -Spoken English  4. Listening.    I. Title.
    PE1128.F569  1994
    428.3'4--dc20                                    93-41028
                                                     CIP

ISBN: 0-8384-5270-1

# CONTENTS

# TO THE TEACHER

English as a Second Language Learners are surrounded by sounds—conversations, announcements, music, television, radio, instructions. Listening is their primary source of language input. Our challenge as teachers is to help students make sense of this incoming stream of language. As learners, our students need practice and listening strategies. As individuals, they need confidence in their ability to understand their new language.

*Now Hear This!* is a listening, pronunciation, and speaking text for high beginning students of ESL. It develops listening skills for high interest narratives and informal conversations. The text and accompanying tapes may be used with college-level students, adult programs, and high school classes. The materials are both easy to use and highly effective in a language laboratory.

*Now Hear This!* is one in a series of three titles designed to develop aural/oral communication skills. The complete series has been designed to meet the needs of students from the beginning to intermediate levels and includes the following:

- *Listen to Me!*        beginning
- *Now Hear This!*       high beginning
- *That Sounds Good!*    intermediate

There are fifteen thematic units in *Now Hear This!* each composed of seven sections. In COMPREHENSION, students listen to a one-to-three minute recorded narrative. They hear the organization of the language and the sequence and relationships of ideas. Then, through a variety of interactive exercises, they learn to listen for general and specific details. In both the STRUCTURE and PRONUNCIATION sections, students concentrate on language discrimination, listening for structure or phonological features such as reductions, elisions, and intonation. The CONVERSATION section presents three to six short conversations or interview comments related to the topic. The interviews are transcriptions of authentic language. The conversations were roleplayed and scripted, with liberal use of expressions and replies that were recorded while gathering natural speech for this text. Students focus on general meaning and listening strategies. The final three sections—INTERVIEWS, FACE TO FACE, and INTERACTION—give students the opportunity to share their own interests and opinions in a variety of settings.

## UNIT ORGANIZATION

### Comprehension

The first part of the unit presents a recorded story, focusing on a particular person, event, or theme. The stories are approximately one to three minutes in length. The exercises in this section provide background and vocabulary for the story, help students follow the story line, and ask students to listen for specific information.

A large photo or illustration introduces the theme of the unit. Teachers should encourage students to comment on the person and/or activities in the picture. For example, for Unit 2, My Mom Smokes, the teacher might ask: Where is this?, What's the woman doing?, Do you think she smokes a lot?, Do you know anyone who smokes?

The *Before You Listen* activity is designed to stimulate student interest in the topic. It may draw out personal opinions about such topics as work, drinking, or dreams. It relates the topic to students' own lives; for example, by asking them to identify the state and area in which they live on the census map or by checking the recycling services offered in their towns. The activity may also draw on students' background information by asking what facts they may know about smoking, famous world events, the World Trade Center, or other topics.

*Key Words* defines several words from the listening passage. Students then complete sentences with the correct word.

In the *First Listening,* students are asked a question, then they listen to the recorded story for the first time. For some classes, it may be helpful to play the tape in sections, a few sentences at a time. After listening, students tell the class any information they remember about the story. The focus here is not on structure, but on the comprehension of the story. One student may only be able to recall one small piece of information. Another may be able to remember many facts. Students who may have had difficulty understanding the selection will learn from their classmates.

After the first listening, students are directed to listen to the selection two more times while working on specific tasks. They may be asked to identify ideas that a speaker mentions, indicate on a map whether the population of certain cities has increased or decreased, check the outlook for specific jobs, put events in order, etc.

In the final activity of this section, *Comprehension,* students hear several questions about the story and circle the correct answers.

## Structure

In the first part of each unit, the emphasis is on content. In the next two sections, the emphasis shifts to listening discrimination. In the first exercise in STRUCTURE, students focus on verb tense. Although there is a variety of tenses within each selection, one tense usually predominates. Students listen to individual sentences from the listening passage and write the complete verb.

There may be a second structure exercise, directing students to listen for features such as tense contrast or negatives.

## Pronunciation

Within each listening selection, a recurring pronunciation feature has been highlighted; for example, *can* and *can't, and* and *or,* the reduction of *h* in *his/him/her,* linking, or stressed syllables. A pronunciation box with a short explanation and one or more examples presents the feature. Students circle the phonological item they hear, complete sentences with the correct word, or mark stress or intonation.

## Conversations

This section begins with three to six short conversations or interview comments related to the topic. The conversations are purposely pitched at a more difficult level than the narratives, so that students begin to realize that they do not need to understand every word in a conversation. In the first exercise, students guess the general meaning by matching the conversation with the picture to which it refers. Often, simply by recognizing a few of the vocabulary words or phrases in the exchange, students will be able to make their selections. The second exercise helps students draw more specific details from the conversation. Further exercises develop listening strategies, helping students to become familiar with common conversation techniques, such as checking or repeating information, asking for a further explanation, or deciding on sentence intonation.

## Interviews / Face to Face / Interaction

In the early sections of each unit, students are involved with listening as a one-way process, listening to stories, narratives, and conversations. In the last three sections, students become involved with listening as a two-way process, interacting as both listener and speaker. In this role, students may ned to ask for repetition or may need to ask questions to clarify meaning.

In INTERVIEWS, there are two identical interview charts. In class, students should sit with a classmate and take turns asking and answering the questions. Students become familiar with the questions, vocabulary, and possible answers. As a second step, students are instructed to conduct the same interview with a friend, neighbor, or co-worker. Stress to students that this interview should be conducted in English. If at all possible, the person being interviewed should be a native speaker of English. The next class after this activity, students should share some of their answers. Discuss the process and talk about any problems they may have had in listening or speaking and the strategies they used to negotiate meaning.

FACE TO FACE is an information-gap activity. Students work as partners. One student (Student A) looks at the page in the unit. The second student (Student B) turns to the FACE TO FACE appendix. Students may not look at one another's information. Only by discussing and working together will students be able to complete the tasks. For example, students are asked to find the differences in two pictures, to complete a map with the population of major cities in the United States, to fill in a chart on the average salaries and job outlook for selected occupations, or to label the parts of a computer.

INTERACTION is a speaking activity that allows students to share personal information, ideas and opinions. Students should sit in small groups, consisting of three to four students so that every student has an opportunity to participate. The topics are open-ended and stimulate discussion. For example, the groups have to decide what a person should do in two emergency situations, draw and explain a recent dream, analyze eight pictured situations, decide how each person could save energy or resources, or decide if smoking should or shouldn't be allowed in specific locations.

## COMPONENTS

*Now Hear This!* is a complete and fully-integrated program for students and teachers alike. Complementing the student text is a series of audio cassettes containing all of the listening passages and follow-up activities. A sample cassette may be obtained free of charge from the publisher.

# ACKNOWLEDGMENTS

In the revised edition of *Now Hear This!*, I was working from a treasure chest. The original text has been used by thousands of students over the past nine years. By listening carefully, I have been able to apply student and teacher feedback plus new research in the ESL field to add, delete, and change features of the existing program. With much appreciation to the individuals below, the revised edition of *Now Hear This!* is hopefully up-to-date, effective and enjoyable to use.

Thank you to my colleagues at Union County College. You've always been available to share ideas, test materials, and speak into a tape recorder. Special thanks to Howard Pomann, Dorothy Burak, Marinna Kolaitis, Liz Neblett, Larry Wollman, John McDermott, Litza Georgiou, and Andre DeSandies. I would also like to recognize Donna Lawless, college librarian, for providing last-minute facts and figures. I am especially grateful for the support of Union County College in granting me a sabbatical in which to complete this project.

The professional staff at Heinle & Heinle compiled program feedback, arranged sharing sessions, and were enthusiastic and supportive throughout the revision of *Now Hear This!* I appreciate the special assistance of Erik Gundersen, Lynne Telson Barsky, and Karen Hazar of Heinle & Heinle, and Anita Raducanu of A+ Publishing Services.

When writing, an author owes a special debt to researchers and theoreticians in the ESL field. Over the past several years, I have read journal articles and books on listening by the following individuals. Additionally, I was privileged to hear all of them speak at International TESOL conferences: Patricia Dunkel, Stephen Krashen, Joan Morley, Pat Wilcox Peterson, Jack Richards, and Penny Ur.

Finally, thank you, Bill, for your constant support and confidence in me.

# Now Hear This!

# Do You Like Your Job?

## COMPREHENSION

**A. Before You Listen** This person is a toll collector. What do you think he likes about his job? What doesn't he like?

1. He likes _____ .

2. He likes _____ .

3. He doesn't like _____ .

4. He doesn't like _____ .

**B. Key Words** Discuss the new vocabulary, then complete the sentences below.

| | |
|---|---|
| **recognize** | to know, to be able to identify |
| **overtime** | extra hours of work, usually paid at a higher hourly rate |
| **token** | a round piece of metal that looks like a coin, often deposited in a machine to pay for using a road, bridge, or bus |
| **lucky** | having good fortune or good things happen |
| **over and over** | again and again |
| **fumes** | smoke or gas, usually from a car |
| **complains** | to say that you are unhappy or not satisfied |
| **promotion** | a better position at work |

1. She was _____ to find a job.

2. I can _____ any car and tell you what year it is.

3. Gas _____ are one cause of pollution.

4. My boss _____ if we take one extra minute at break time.

5. My friend received a _____ ; she's now the manager.

6. My work is boring. I do the same thing _____ .

7. Last week, I worked five hours _____ .

8. The toll is fifty cents. If you use a _____ , it's only forty cents.

▭ **C. First Listening** Listen to two people talk about their jobs as toll collectors. Who likes the job? Who doesn't like the job? After you listen, tell the class any other information you remember about the story.

▭ **D. Second Listening** Listen to each speaker again. Circle the ideas they talk about.

| *Speaker 1* | | *Speaker 2* | |
|---|---|---|---|
| hours | coworkers | hours | coworkers |
| boss | benefits | boss | benefits |
| overtime | promotions | overtime | promotions |
| pay | | pay | |

▭ **E. Like / Doesn't like** You will hear ten sentences. Decide if the speaker is describing something he likes or doesn't like about his job.

1. like    doesn't like          6. like    doesn't like
2. like    doesn't like          7. like    doesn't like
3. like    doesn't like          8. like    doesn't like
4. like    doesn't like          9. like    doesn't like
5. like    doesn't like         10. like    doesn't like

# STRUCTURE

▭ **A. Present Tense** Listen to these sentences. Write the present tense verb you hear.

1. _____hate_____          6. _____
2. _____          7. _____
3. _____          8. _____
4. _____          9. _____
5. _____         10. _____

▭ **B. Always / Never** Look at the explanation about the placement of *always* and *never*. Read the sentences on page 5. Stop the tape and put a star (*) at the correct place for *always* or *never*. Then, listen to the sentences and check your answers.

---

*Always* **and** *Never*

Put *always* and *never* after the verb *to be*.

    My boss **is** *never* satisfied with my work.

Put *always* and *never* before the verb.

    He *always* **complains** about my work.

---

1.  I work overtime.  (never)
2.  I am late for work.  (never)
3.  The boss complains about my work.  (always)
4.  The boss gives me good evaluations.  (always)
5.  I am bored at work.  (never)
6.  I am tired after eight hours.  (always)
7.  The boss is satisfied with my work.  (never)
8.  I enjoy talking with people.  (always)
9.  I am going to quit this job.  (never)
10.  The boss gives me overtime.  (never)

# PRONUNCIATION

**A. *And / Or*** Listen carefully and complete these sentences with *and* or *or*.

> *And* often sounds like *ānd*. *Or* often sounds like *ŏr*.
> My hands and feet are cold.
> I can't see my family or friends.

1.  I sit _____ stand.
2.  I usually work on Saturday _____ Sunday.
3.  I can recognize every make _____ model.
4.  I sometimes see a Lambourghini _____ a Rolls Royce.
5.  I have medical benefits for myself _____ my family.
6.  I collect money _____ a token.
7.  It's the same thing over _____ over.
8.  I work eight _____ nine hours a night.
9.  In the winter, the work is cold _____ boring.
10.  I'm going to quit _____ find a new job.

**B. *Don't*** In spoken English, it is sometimes difficult to hear *don't*. Listen carefully and circle the sentence you hear.

1.  a.  I like my job.                          b.  I don't like my job.
2.  a.  I work a lot of overtime.               b.  I don't work a lot of overtime.
3.  a.  I think the work is interesting.        b.  I don't think the work is interesting.
4.  a.  I have medical benefits.                b.  I don't have medical benefits.
5.  a.  I work during the day.                  b.  I don't work during the day.
6.  a.  I like to work in the cold weather.     b.  I don't like to work in the cold weather.
7.  a.  I want to stay here.                     b.  I don't want to stay here.
8.  a.  I need to look for another job.          b.  I don't need to look for another job.

# CONVERSATIONS

🔲 **A. Match** Listen to these people talk about their jobs. Write the number of the conversation on the correct picture. Write one thing that the person likes about the job. Write one thing that the person doesn't like about the job.

He likes _____ .

He doesn't like _____ .

She likes _____ .

She doesn't like _____ .

He likes _____ .

He doesn't like _____ .

She likes _____ .

She doesn't like _____ .

🔲 **B. True or False** Listen to each conversation again. Write *T* if the sentence is true, *F* if the sentence is false.

*Conversation 1*

1. _____ This person works and goes to school.

2. _____ This person works the same time every week.

*Conversation 2*

3. _____ This person has medical benefits now.

4. _____ This company gives medical benefits to all employees and their families.

*Conversation 3*

5. _____ This woman is the only female salesperson at this car dealer.

6. _____ All of the men are friendly to her.

*Conversation 4*

7. _____ This person works alone.

8. _____ This person works a lot of weekends.

📼   **C. How**   Listen to these *How* questions. Circle the appropriate answer.

1. a. I like it a lot.
   b. I'm a telephone operator.
2. a. She's helpful.
   b. She's a woman.
3. a. If I want, I can work overtime.
   b. They're terrible. I work from 11 P.M. to 7 A.M.
4. a. They're great. I have health insurance for me and my family.
   b. Yes, I have benefits.
5. a. There are twenty people.
   b. They're friendly.
6. a. It's a little slow.
   b. It's called United Car Rentals.

## INTERVIEWS

**In-Class Interview**   Interview a classmate about his or her job.

| | |
|---|---|
| 1. Where do you work? | |
| 2. What do you do? | |
| 3. What are your hours? | |
| 4. What benefits do you have? | |
| 5. Do you ever work overtime? | |
| 6. What do you like about your job? | |
| 7. What don't you like about your job? | |
| 8. How did you find this job? | |
| 9. How long have you been working there? | |

**Out-Of-Class Interview**   Interview a friend or neighbor about his or her job.

| | |
|---|---|
| 1. Where do you work? | |
| 2. What do you do? | |
| 3. What are your hours? | |
| 4. What benefits do you have? | |
| 5. Do you ever work overtime? | |
| 6. What do you like about your job? | |
| 7. What don't you like about your job? | |
| 8. How did you find this job? | |
| 9. How long have you been working there? | |

# FACE TO FACE

STUDENT A: The incomplete chart below gives information about four people and their jobs. Student B has the missing information. Ask and answer questions about these four people. Complete the information.

STUDENT B: Turn to page 131.

1.

PLACE: ___Maxwell's___
JOB: _____
HOURS: ___4 P.M. to 12 A.M.___
SALARY: _____
BENEFITS: ___none___
OPINION: ___He likes the job, not the hours.___

2.

PLACE: _____
JOB: ___engineer___
HOURS: ___9 A.M. to 5 P.M.___
SALARY: _____
BENEFITS: ___medical, 4 weeks vacation___
OPINION: _____

3.

PLACE: ___Summit Hospital___
JOB: _____
HOURS: _____
SALARY: ___$25,000 a year___
BENEFITS: _____
OPINION: ___She likes the job a lot.___

4.

PLACE: _____
JOB: ___librarian___
HOURS: _____
SALARY: ___$32,000 a year___
BENEFITS: ___medical, 3 weeks vacation___
OPINION: _____

## Helpful Language

Where does he work?

What does he do?

What hours does he work?

What's his salary?

What benefits does he have?

Does he like his job?

## INTERACTION

Sit in a small group and look at these classified ads from the newspaper. Answer the questions below.

1. Which jobs require experience?
2. Which jobs require a special license or certificate?
3. Which jobs require a college education?

Check two or three jobs that you are interested in. Give your reasons to your group.

---

**ACCOUNTANT** – Small firm needs accountant with 3+ years of public accounting exp. Plan and supervise audits and reviews. Strong computer skills. All benefits. Fax resume to 908-371-6434.

**AUTO MECHANIC** Experienced in brakes, mufflers, tune-ups and general repairs. Day hours. Call Al at 329-9638.

**BURGLAR ALARM INSTALLER** — Great opportunity to learn from the beginning. We will train you in the security alarm business. Must be high school grad and have own car. Call 698-8496.

**BUS DRIVER** Part time. Small private school. Special license required. Call 907-4433.

**DATA ENTRY** Small accounting firm needs data entry person with computer skills. P/T, 20 hours a wk. $8 an hour. Call Mr. Fox at 654-0809.

**ELECTRICIAN** Minimum 5 years exp. in residential and commercial wiring. Good benefits. 553-2233.

**FLORAL DESIGNER** Must have flower shop experience. F/T position. 558-9191.

**INSURANCE PROCESSOR** Person to work in doctor's office. Exp. in processing medical claims and billing. 343-9212.

**LAB TECHNICIAN** Large health clinic is seeking a licensed lab technician with 2 yrs. exp. Bilingual a plus. Excellent benefits. Send resume to City Health Center, Center Plaza, Newton, MA 02156.

**MANICURIST** Excellent employment for manicurist in new salon in shopping mall. One year experience. Call Joyce at 667-1188.

**MEDICAL OFFICE ASSISTANT** P/T Good typing, good spelling, filing. Bilingual, Spanish/English 322-1156.

**PHYSICAL THERAPIST** Full time registered physical therapist for rehabilitation center. Excellent benefits. 845-8338.

**PLUMBER** Plumbing, heating, air-conditioning technician. Driver's license and exp. required. 544-9112.

**RADIATION THERAPIST** F/T Mon.-Fri. New facility. 2 yrs. exp. Call Easton Hospital. 233-1400.

**REAL ESTATE** Major real estate firm looking for real estate salespeople. License required. No exp. necessary. 343-0807.

**SECURITY OFFICERS** Full and p/t positions. Excellent pay and working conditions. Car and home phone necessary. Call 237-8978.

# MY MOM SMOKES

## COMPREHENSION

**A. Before You Listen** Guess if the following statements about smoking are true or false. Write *T* if the statement is true, *F* if the statement is false. (Check your answers on page 129.)

1. _____ About one out of every ten Americans smokes.

2. _____ The number one cause of death by cancer for both men and women is lung cancer.

3. _____ About 15,000 Americans a year die of lung cancer.

4. _____ Every day, about three thousand young people begin to smoke.

5. _____ Children who breathe their parents' smoke have more coughs, colds, and ear problems.

6. _____ Smoking during pregnancy may cause premature birth.

**B. Key Words** Discuss the new vocabulary, then complete the sentences below.

| | |
|---|---|
| **as soon as** | at the moment that; when |
| **lounge** | a room at work where people sit or take a break |
| **smells** | to have a bad odor |
| **short of breath** | not able to breathe easily |
| **cough** | the act of sending out air from the lungs with a loud sound |
| **quit** | to stop |
| **hypnotized** | to put in a sleeplike condition |

1. My sister smokes. Her teeth are stained and her breath always

   _____ .

2. He lights up a cigarette _____ he wakes up.

3. He's a heavy smoker. He gets _____ when he climbs the stairs.

4. I stopped smoking after I was _____ .

5. I'm going to _____ smoking when I have children.

6. Your _____ sounds terrible. When are you going to stop smoking?

7. The only place we can smoke at work is in the employees' _____ .

**C. First Listening** Read these sentences. Then listen to the story. Check the times that this woman smokes. After you listen, tell the class any other information you remember about the story.

_____ 1. when she wakes up     _____ 4. at the office

_____ 2. when she eats     _____ 5. in the employees' lounge

_____ 3. when she drives     _____ 6. when she watches TV

**D. Second Listening** This woman's family wants her to stop smoking. Listen again and write three reasons her daughter gives. Only write two or three words for each reason.

1. _____

2. _____

3. _____

**E. Comprehension Questions** Listen and circle the correct answer.

1. a. two or three
   b. five or six
   c. a pack or more

2. a. Employees can only smoke in their offices.
   b. Employees can smoke anywhere.
   c. Employees can only smoke in the employees' lounge.

3. a. surprised
   b. angry
   c. worried

4. a. Yes.
   b. No.

5. a. She spends too much money on cigarettes.
   b. The house smells.
   c. She is hurting her children's health.

6. a. She has very little energy.
   b. She coughs all the time.
   c. She has cancer.

7. a. Yes.
   b. No.

# STRUCTURE

**A. Tense Contrast** Listen to these sentences. Decide the tense of the verb. Circle _present_ or _past_.

1. present     past        6. present     past

2. present     past        7. present     past

3. present     past        8. present     past

4. present     past        9. present     past

5. present     past       10. present     past

**B. Negatives** Listen to these sentences. Write the negative verb.

1. Her family _____ her to smoke.
2. She _____ at her desk.
3. She _____ a lot of energy.
4. She _____ how to stop.
5. Her children _____ .
6. Her husband _____ .
7. The children _____ her to smoke.
8. She _____ .
9. The children _____ the smell of smoke.
10. _____ to smoke.

# PRONUNCIATION

**A. Same or Different** You will hear two verbs. Decide if they are the same or different. Circle *same* or *different*.

| | | | | | |
|---|---|---|---|---|---|
| 1. same | different | | 6. same | different |
| 2. same | different | | 7. same | different |
| 3. same | different | | 8. same | different |
| 4. same | different | | 9. same | different |
| 5. same | different | | 10. same | different |

**B. Linking with -s** Listen carefully and complete these sentences with the missing words. Mark the linking sounds.

> When a final **-s** is followed by a vowel, the sounds are linked.
> The **-s** sounds like part of the next word.
>    My mom **has a** problem.

1. My mom _smokes a_ lot.
2. She always _____ ____ cigarette in her hand.
3. She _____ ____ day.
4. She _____ ____ soon as she _____ ____.
5. She _____ _____ a cigarette after breakfast.
6. She _____ ____ an office.
7. She _____ ____ the employees' lounge.
8. She _____ _____ pack of cigarettes a day.
9. My little sister _____ _____ the time.
10. My mom _____ ____ bed.

# CONVERSATIONS

🔲 **A. Match** Listen to these conversations. In each of them, one person is asking another person not to smoke. Write the number of the conversation on the correct picture.

🔲 **B. Same or Different** Read each sentence. Then, listen and decide if the meaning is the same or different. Circle *S* or *D*.

S   D   1. You can smoke in my office.

S   D   2. I only want one.

S   D   3. This is the only place I can smoke.

S   D   4. We can put the windows in the car down.

S   D   5. Now you can't.

S   D   6. I can smoke here now.

**C. Smoking Situations** You will hear some common questions that smokers and non-smokers ask. How would you answer?

1. a. Yes.
   b. No.
2. a. Sure, go ahead.
   b. Please don't.
3. a. No problem.
   b. Well, I'd rather you didn't.
4. a. Thanks.
   b. No. I don't smoke.

5. a. Sure.
   b. Why? I can smoke here.
6. a. I don't smoke.
   b. Sure. Have one.
7. a. Sorry.
   b. Sure.
8. a. Smoking.
   b. Non-smoking.

# INTERVIEWS

**In-Class Interview** Interview a classmate about smoking regulations in another country.

| | |
|---|---|
| 1. What country are you from? | |
| 2. How old do you have to be to buy a pack of cigarettes? | |
| 3. Are young people warned against smoking? | |
| 4. Is there a warning label on cigarettes? | |
| 5. Are cigarettes advertised on television? | |
| 6. Are cigarettes advertised in magazines and newspapers? | |
| 7. Is there a national campaign against smoking? | |
| 8. Where is smoking allowed? | |
| 9. Where isn't smoking allowed? | |

**Out-of-Class Interview** Interview an American about smoking regulations in the United States.

| | |
|---|---|
| 1. How old do you have to be to buy a pack of cigarettes in the United States? | |
| 2. Are young people warned against smoking? | |
| 3. Is there a warning label on cigarettes? | |
| 4. Are cigarettes advertised on television? | |
| 5. Are cigarettes advertised in magazines and newspapers? | |
| 6. Is there a national campaign against smoking? | |
| 7. Where is smoking allowed? | |
| 8. Where isn't smoking allowed? | |

## FACE TO FACE

STUDENT A: Look at the chart below. Student B will read ten sentences about smoking. Decide if you agree or disagree with each statement. Check *Agree* or *Disagree* and tell your partner how you feel. Change roles. Turn to page 132 and read the sentences.

STUDENT B: Turn to page 132.

When you both finish, discuss the statements that you don't have the same opinion about. Give your reasons.

| Statement | Agree | Disagree |
|:---:|:---:|:---:|
| 1 | | |
| 2 | | |
| 3 | | |
| 4 | | |
| 5 | | |
| 6 | | |
| 7 | | |
| 8 | | |
| 9 | | |
| 10 | | |

### Helpful Language

I agree completely.

I feel the same.

Definitely.

Absolutely.

That's just what I think.

I don't agree with that.

I don't think that's right.

I don't think so.

That's wrong.

# INTERACTION

Smoking is not allowed in many public offices and buildings. It is not allowed on domestic airline flights. Many restaurants now have smoking and non-smoking sections. Sit with a group of three or four students. As a committee, you must decide if smoking should or should not be allowed in the places below. Give your reasons.

1.

Smoking _____   No Smoking _____

Reason _____

_____

2.

Smoking _____   No Smoking _____

Reason _____

_____

3.

Smoking _____   No Smoking _____

Reason _____

_____

4.

Smoking _____   No Smoking _____

Reason _____

_____

# ADULT DAY CARE

## COMPREHENSION

**A. Before You Listen** These are the eight places a senior citizen is most likely to visit during the week. Check the three places you think that senior citizens go most frequently. (Check your answers on page 129.)

_____ a movie                    _____ church or synagogue

_____ a store                    _____ the library

_____ a senior citizens' center  _____ a doctor

_____ the home of a relative or friend   _____ a restaurant

**B. Key Words** Discuss the new vocabulary, then complete the sentences below.

| | |
|---|---|
| **patient** | a person under a doctor's care or in the hospital |
| **participating** | taking an active part in |
| **elderly** | old, usually a person who is over 80 |
| **recovered** | to get better after an illness or accident |
| **physical therapy** | treatment and exercise to help a patient return to normal movement after an accident or illness |
| **stroke** | a lack of oxygen to the brain which could leave a person paralyzed or weak |
| **valuable** | important |

1. He needed _____ to help him walk again after his accident.

2. After my mother had a _____ , she couldn't move the left side of her body.

3. My father _____ quickly after his accident. He was home from the hospital in ten days.

4. Many families are _____ in this program.

5. This program is _____ for both patients and their families.

6. The woman who lives above me is _____ ; she's over 90.

7. After her operation, she was a _____ in the hospital for two weeks.

**C. First Listening** Listen to this story about adult day care. What is adult day care? Why are David Brown and Ann Ramos in this program? After you listen, tell the class any other information you remember about the story.

**D. Second Listening** Listen to the story again. Check the activities and services that this adult day-care center offers.

_____ 1. physical therapy      _____ 6. painting

_____ 2. lunch      _____ 7. driving lessons

_____ 3. friendship      _____ 8. sewing

_____ 4. swimming      _____ 9. games

_____ 5. baseball      _____ 10. cooking

**E. Comprehension Questions** Listen and circle the correct answer.

1. a. He started a fire in their apartment.
   b. She doesn't want to stay with him all day.
   c. She's worried that he might hurt himself.

2. a. Ann sits next to her daughter when she reads.
   b. Ann follows her out of the house when she takes out the garbage.
   c. Ann doesn't know what to do all day.

3. a. at home
   b. in the hospital
   c. in the center

4. a. half days
   b. every day
   c. five days a week

5. a. sewing
   b. talking with one another
   c. painting

6. a. They are elderly.
   b. They had strokes.
   c. They are becoming forgetful.

7. a. Family members can continue to work.
   b. Family members can have a break.
   c. both **a** and **b**

## STRUCTURE

**A. Present Tense** Listen to these sentences. Write the present tense verb you hear.

1. _____lives_____        6. _____

2. _____        7. _____

3. _____        8. _____

4. _____        9. _____

5. _____        10. _____

## PRONUNCIATION

**A. Linking with -s** Listen carefully and complete these sentences with the missing words. Mark the linking sounds.

> When a final **-s** is followed by a vowel, the sounds are linked.
> The **-s** sounds like part of the next word.
>      Mr. Brown **participates in** the program.

1. David Brown _____ _____ home.

2. He _____ _____ home all day.

3. His wife _____ _____ an office.

4. She _____ _____ her husband.

5. He _____ _____ little things in the house.

6. Ann Ramos _____ _____ the program, too.

7. She _____ _____ break.

8. She only _____ _____ the morning.

9. Ann _____ _____ plays cards with her friends.

10. The program _____ _____ for the elderly.

**B. Is / Does**  Circle the answer to these questions. Listen carefully for
*Is he, Is she, Does he,* or *Does she.*

> We often do not hear the **h** in questions that begin with *Is* or *Does.*
> Is he — Ishe        Does he — Doeshe

1.  Yes, he is.        Yes, she is.        Yes, he does.        Yes, she does.
2.  Yes, he is.        Yes, she is.        Yes, he does.        Yes, she does.
3.  Yes, he is.        Yes, she is.        Yes, he does.        Yes, she does.
4.  Yes, he is.        Yes, she is.        Yes, he does.        Yes, she does.
5.  Yes, he is.        Yes, she is.        Yes, he does.        Yes, she does.
6.  Yes, he is.        Yes, she is.        Yes, he does.        Yes, she does.
7.  Yes, he is.        Yes, she is.        Yes, he does.        Yes, she does.
8.  Yes, he is.        Yes, she is.        Yes, he does.        Yes, she does.
9.  Yes, he is.        Yes, she is.        Yes, he does.        Yes, she does.
10. Yes, he is.        Yes, she is.        Yes, he does.        Yes, she does.

## SPEAKERS

**A. Match**  Write the number of the conversation on the correct picture.

**B. Listen and Check**  Senior citizens report that they spend a lot of time on these activities. Listen to each speaker again. Check the activities they talk about.

| Activity | 1 | 2 | 3 | 4 | 5 | 6 |
|---|---|---|---|---|---|---|
| Caring for a spouse or relative | | | | | | |
| Spending time with friends and family | | | | | | |
| Enjoying recreational activities | | | | | | |
| Reading | | | | | | |
| Walking / Exercising | | | | | | |
| Watching TV | | | | | | |
| Volunteering | | | | | | |
| Going to a senior citizens' center | | | | | | |
| Working | | | | | | |

**C. _How often_**  Listen again. Answer these questions about how often each person participates in the following activities.

1.  How often does she go to the library?

    _____

    How often does she play cards with her friends?

    _____

2.  How often does he work at the butcher shop?

    _____

    How often does he work in his woodshop?

    _____

3.  How often does she see her son?

    _____

4.  How often does she exercise in the pool?

    _____

    How often does she walk?

    _____

5.  How often does he go to the park?

    _____

    How often does he go to a show or a concert?

    _____

6.  How often does she go to the supermarket?

    _____

    How often does she visit her son?

    _____

## INTERVIEWS

**In-Class Interview** Interview a classmate about an elderly relative.

| | |
|---|---|
| 1. Do you have an elderly relative? | |
| 2. How old is she? | |
| 3. Where does she live? | |
| 4. Does she live alone? | |
| 5. Is she healthy? | |
| 6. What does she do during the day? | |
| 7. How does she get around? | |
| 8. Does she get any exercise? | |
| 9. How often do you visit this person? | |

**Out-of-Class Interview** Interview a friend, neighbor, or coworker about an elderly relative.

| | |
|---|---|
| 1. Do you have an elderly relative? | |
| 2. How old is he? | |
| 3. Where does he live? | |
| 4. Does he live alone? | |
| 5. Is he healthy? | |
| 6. What does he do during the day? | |
| 7. How does he get around? | |
| 8. Does he get any exercise? | |
| 9. How often do you visit this person? | |

## 👥 FACE TO FACE

STUDENT A: Read numbers 1 to 8 and circle the answers you think are correct. Then check your answers with Student B. Begin each question with the words in parentheses. Then, change roles. Student B will ask you about numbers 9 to 16.

STUDENT B: Turn to page 133.

1. _____ live longer. (Who?)
   a. men      b. women

2. The life expectancy for men is _____ . (What?)
   a. 70      b. 72      c. 75

3. The life expectancy for women is _____ . (What?)
   a. 70      b. 75      c. 80

4. _____ has the highest life expectancy. (Which country?)
   a. Japan      b. the United States      c. Canada

5. _____ of the population of the U.S. is over 65.
   (What percentage?)
   a. five percent      b. thirteen percent      c. twenty percent

6. _____ has the highest number of senior citizens.
   (Which state?)
   a. New York      b. Florida      c. California

7. _____ has the highest percentage of senior citizens.
   (Which state?)
   a. Florida      b. Texas      c. Pennsylvania

8. Most senior citizens live _____ . (Where?)
   a. at home      b. with a relative      c. in their own homes

9. The major source of income for people over 65 is *Social Security*.

10. Most senior citizens describe their health as *good*.

11. The most common medical condition for seniors is *arthritis*.

12. Most senior citizens see their children *once a week*.

13. *About four percent* of the elderly live in nursing homes.

14. The favorite leisure-time activity for seniors is *watching TV*.

15. The most common cause of death for senior citizens is *heart disease*.

16. Senior citizens say their biggest problem is *the high cost of living*.

# APARTMENT PROBLEMS

## COMPREHENSION

**A. Before You Listen** Complete this information about a problem you had in your apartment or home. Talk about your answers with the class.

1. Where do you live?     ___ I live in a house.

   ___ I live in an apartment.

   ___ I live in a dorm.

2. Who do you call when you have a problem in your home?

   ___ I call the manager / landlord / super.

   ___ I call a repair person.

**B. Key Words** Discuss the new vocabulary, then complete the sentences below.

| | |
|---|---|
| **expecting** | to be pregnant |
| **landlord / landlady** | a person who manages an apartment building |
| **mess** | not in order, dirty |
| **stuck** | not able to open |
| **radiator** | a unit that radiates or conducts heat |
| **overflowing** | to flow up and over, especially water |
| **leaking** | to drip or escape through a hole or a crack |

1. I can't open the door. It's _____ .

2. It's cold in this room. The _____ isn't turned on.

3. Theresa is pregnant. She's _____ her first child in two months.

4. The toilet is stopped up. Water is _____ onto the floor.

5. Nothing is clean and clothes are all over the floor. This room is a _____ .

6. There's a problem in the bathroom upstairs. Water is _____ through the ceiling into the living room.

7. I call the _____ when I have a problem with the heat.

▭ **C. First Listening** Look at the picture on page 26 and listen to this story about looking for an apartment. There are six problems in this apartment. As you listen, number each problem on the picture. After you listen, tell the class any other information you remember about the story.

▭ **D. Second Listening** Listen to the story again. Write the six problems as you listen to the tape. Only write two or three words for each problem.

1. _____ *oven – smoking* _____
2. _____
3. _____
4. _____
5. _____
6. _____

▭ **E. Comprehension Questions** Listen and circle the correct answer.

1. a. It's very big.
   b. It's a one-bedroom apartment.
   c. It's a two-bedroom apartment.

2. a. Theresa is expecting a baby.
   b. in Chicago
   c. in two months

3. a. today
   b. next week
   c. in two months

4. a. It doesn't work.
   b. It's stuck.
   c. It's a mess.

5. a. It doesn't work.
   b. There's a problem in the apartment above this one.
   c. Charles can't turn the water off.

6. a. There are a lot of problems.
   b. Yes, he probably will.
   c. No, he probably won't.

7. a. The rent is too high.
   b. They don't want to rent this apartment.
   c. Theresa is going to have the baby.

## STRUCTURE

**A. Present Continuous Tense**  Listen to these sentences. Write the present continuous verb you hear.

1. _____is expecting_____   6. _____

2. _____   7. _____

3. _____   8. _____

4. _____   9. _____

5. _____   10. _____

**B. Tense Contrast**  Listen to these sentences. Decide if they are about now or the future. Circle *now* or *future*.

1.  now    future    6.  now    future

2.  now    future    7.  now    future

3.  now    future    8.  now    future

4.  now    future    9.  now    future

5.  now    future    10.  now    future

## PRONUNCIATION

**A. Syllables**  Listen to these words. Write the number of syllables you hear on the line after each word.

| One syllable | Two syllables | Three syllables |
| --- | --- | --- |
| week | landlord | apartment |
| door | baby | Chicago |
| light | building | probably |

1. live ____    6. problem ____    11. around ____

2. larger ____    7. expecting ____    12. stuck ____

3. Theresa ____    8. leaking ____    13. rent ____

4. air ____    9. smoking ____    14. overflow ____

5. ceiling ____    10. family ____    15. fix ____

**B. Can / Can't** Listen to these sentences. Write *can* or *can't* and the main verb.

> *Can* is pronounced *cán*. The main verb is stressed.
>     He can see. — He cán sée.
> *Can't* is pronounced *cán't.* Usually, we don't hear the *t.*
> Both *can't* and the main verb are stressed.
>     He can't see. — He cán't sée.

1.  They _____ _____ the mess.
2.  He _____ _____ off the water.
3.  She _____ _____ the door.
4.  He _____ _____ too well.
5.  They _____ _____ at other apartments.
6.  They _____ _____ in their apartment for another month.
7.  They _____ _____ an apartment they like.
8.  They _____ _____ a real estate agency.
9.  They _____ _____ with Theresa's family for a few months.
10. They _____ _____ $500 rent; they _____ _____ $600.

# CONVERSATIONS

**A. Match** Jack Grimes is the superintendent of a large apartment building. He always receives a lot of calls on Monday morning. Listen to these conversations. Write the number of the conversation on the correct picture.

_____    _____    _____

_____    _____    _____

🔲 **B. Day and Time**  Listen to each conversation again.  On the line under each problem, write the day or time that Mr. Grimes will take care of the problem.

🔲 **C. Repeat the Last Word**  When people are upset, they often repeat the last word or phrase in a sentence. The intonation is the same as for a surprise or a question. Listen to these examples:

◣ **Example 1:**

**A: I'll be there tomorrow.**

**B: Tomorrow! I need you here today.**

◣ **Example 2:**

**A: I'll fix it at 5:00.**

**B: At 5:00? But I don't have any water!**

Now, listen to these sentences. Write the last word or phrase you hear.

1. _____! I need you here now.

2. _____? We don't have any water!

3. _____! How am I supposed to cook?

4. _____? We don't have any electricity!

5. _____! I need a plumber here today.

6. _____? How am I supposed to take a shower?

7. _____! You need to look at it now.

8. _____? We don't have any heat!

9. _____! I need you right now.

10. _____? We don't have any hot water!

## INTERVIEWS

**In-Class Interview**  Interview a classmate about a repair problem.

| | |
|---|---|
| 1. Where do you live? | |
| 2. Did you ever have a problem in your home? | |
| 3. What was the problem? | |
| 4. Who did you call? | |
| 5. How long did you wait for the repair? | |
| 6. Who paid for it? | |

**Out-of-Class Interview**  Interview a friend, neighbor, or coworker about a repair problem.

| | |
|---|---|
| 1. Where do you live? | |
| 2. Did you ever have a problem in your home? | |
| 3. What was the problem? | |
| 4. Who did you call? | |
| 5. How long did you wait for the repair? | |
| 6. Who paid for it? | |

## 👥 FACE TO FACE

STUDENT A: The chart below gives information about Apartment 1. Student B has the information about Apartment 2. Ask and answer questions about the apartments. Complete the missing information.

STUDENT B: Turn to page 134.

| | Apartment 1 | Apartment 2 |
|---|---|---|
| Address | 320 Grove Street | |
| Bedrooms | 2 | |
| Baths | 2 | |
| Rent | $700 a month | |
| Utilities | included | |

***Helpful Language***

Where is the apartment?

How many bedrooms are there?

How many bathrooms are there?

What's the rent?

Are the utilities included?

Please repeat that.

Please repeat the address.

Excuse me. (repeat the question)

## INTERACTION

Sit with a partner. Practice several conversations between a tenant and the manager of the apartment below. The tenant will call and describe one of the problems. The manager will agree to fix the problem. Decide on the time and date for the repair. Change roles.

Act out one of your dialogues in front of the class.

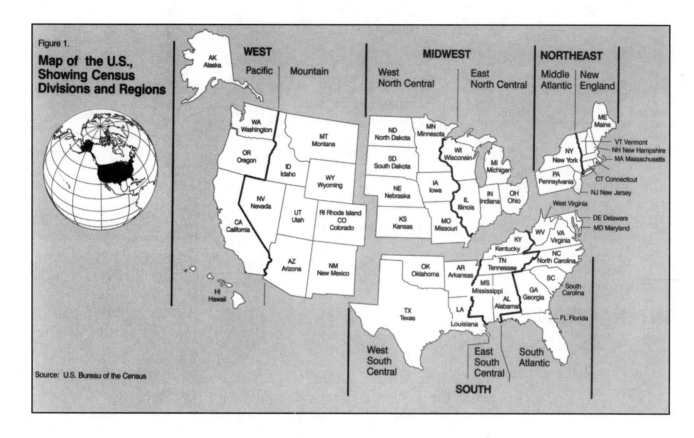

Figure 1.

**Map of the U.S., Showing Census Divisions and Regions**

WEST

Pacific | Mountain

MIDWEST

West North Central | East North Central

NORTHEAST

Middle Atlantic | New England

AK Alaska

WA Washington
OR Oregon
NV Nevada
CA California
ID Idaho
MT Montana
WY Wyoming
UT Utah
AZ Arizona
CO Colorado
RI Rhode Island
NM New Mexico
HI Hawaii

ND North Dakota
SD South Dakota
NE Nebraska
KS Kansas
MN Minnesota
IA Iowa
MO Missouri
WI Wisconsin
IL Illinois
IN Indiana
MI Michigan
OH Ohio

ME Maine
VT Vermont
NH New Hampshire
MA Massachusetts
NY New York
PA Pennsylvania
CT Connecticut
NJ New Jersey
West Virginia
DE Delaware
MD Maryland

KY Kentucky
WV
VA Virginia
TN Tennessee
NC North Carolina
SC South Carolina
GA Georgia
FL Florida

OK Oklahoma
AR Arkansas
MS Mississippi
AL Alabama
TX Texas
LA Louisiana

West South Central | East South Central | South Atlantic

SOUTH

Source: U.S. Bureau of the Census

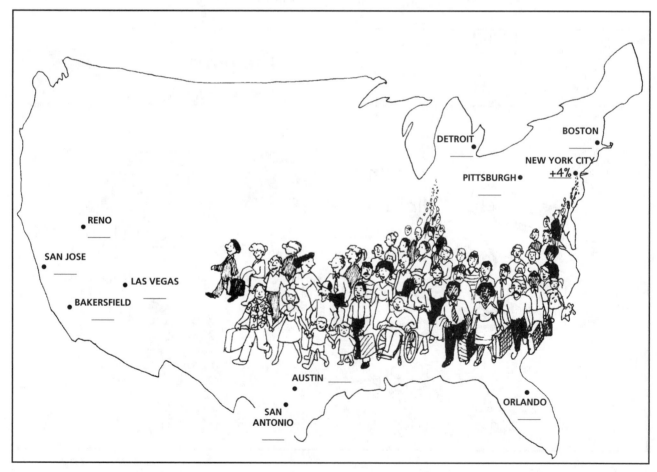

DETROIT
BOSTON
NEW YORK CITY
+4%
PITTSBURGH

RENO
SAN JOSE
LAS VEGAS
BAKERSFIELD

AUSTIN
SAN ANTONIO
ORLANDO

# A Nation on the Move

## COMPREHENSION

**A. Before You Listen**  Look at the map at the top of page 34 and discuss these questions with the class.

> What state do you live in?
>
> What area do you live in?
>
> Are you thinking about moving to another area?
>
> If so, tell which area and give your reasons.

**B. Key Words**  Discuss the new vocabulary, then complete the sentences below.

| | |
|---|---|
| **population** | the number of people who live in an area |
| **residents** | the people who live in a town or state |
| **up** | to be greater or more |
| **declines** | to go down in number or amount |
| **down** | to be smaller or less |
| **retire** | to stop work, usually at the age of 65 |
| **settle** | to go to an area and live there |

1. The _____ of Alaska is 570,000.

2. There are 25,000 _____ in our town.

3. When they _____ , they're going to move to Florida.

4. The population of a town _____ when a major company closes.

5. Many new immigrants _____ in California.

6. The population of Florida is _____ because many people are moving there.

7. The population of the Northeast is _____ because many factories are closing or leaving.

**C. First Listening**  Look at the map at the bottom of page 34 and listen to this story about the census. Which areas of the United States are increasing in population? Which areas are declining? After you listen, tell the class any other information you remember about the story.

**D. Second Listening** Listen to the story again. Decide which area(s) of the country each sentence refers to. Circle *North*, *East*, *South*, or *West*.

1. These areas are declining in population.    North East South West

2. These areas are growing in population.    North East South West

3. Many industries are closing or moving.    North East South West

4. Machines do most of the work on the farms.    North East South West

5. Most new jobs are in these areas.    North East South West

6. These are popular retirement areas.    North East South West

7. Many new immigrants settle here.    North East South West

**E. Map Activity** Look at the map at the bottom of page 34. Listen to this population information from the story. Indicate on the map how much the population of each city is up (+) or down (−). Look at New York City as an example.

**F. Comprehension Questions** Listen and circle the correct answer.

1. a. every year
   b. every five years
   c. every ten years

2. a. Pittsburgh
   b. Detroit
   c. Las Vegas

3. a. Boston
   b. Pittsburgh
   c. Orlando

4. a. from the North to the South
   b. from the South to the West
   c. from the Midwest to the North

5. a. There are less people.
   b. Machines do most of the work on farms.
   c. Many businesses are closing or moving.

6. a. They're tired of their jobs.
   b. They want to live in large cities.
   c. They're looking for a warmer climate.

7. a. in 1990
   b. in 2000
   c. in 2010

# STRUCTURE

**A. Present Continuous Tense** Listen to these sentences. Write the present continuous verb you hear.

1. _____are living_____       6. _____
2. _____          7. _____
3. _____          8. _____
4. _____          9. _____
5. _____          10. _____

# PRONUNCIATION

**A. Stressed Syllables** Listen and mark the stressed syllable.

> In a two-syllable word, one syllable is stressed. It is longer and louder.
>
> a. condúct          c. pícture
> b. cénsus           d. todáy

| | | |
|---|---|---|
| 1. people | 6. reason | 11. country |
| 2. number | 7. decide | 12. decline |
| 3. retire | 8. before | 13. machine |
| 4. because | 9. moving | 14. teacher |
| 5. city | 10. million | 15. settle |

**B. Numbers** This is a chart of the population of the United States from 1900 to 1990. Listen and complete the information. You will hear each sentence twice.

| Year | Population | Year | Population |
|------|-----------|------|-----------|
| 1900 | 76,100,000 | 1950 | |
| 1910 | 92,400,000 | 1960 | |
| 1920 | | 1970 | |
| 1930 | | 1980 | |
| 1940 | | 1990 | |

# CONVERSATIONS

▭ **A. Stay or Move** Listen to these conversations about how people feel about the area they are living in. Decide if the speaker is going to stay in the same area or to move. Check *Stay* or *Move*.

| Conversation | Stay | Move |
|:---:|:---:|:---:|
| 1 | _____ | _____ |
| 2 | _____ | _____ |
| 3 | _____ | _____ |
| 4 | _____ | _____ |
| 5 | _____ | _____ |
| 6 | _____ | _____ |

▭ **B. Place and Reason** Listen to the conversations again. Write the city or state where each person is living now. In one or two words, write the reason this person wants to stay or move.

| Conversation | Place | Reason |
|:---:|:---:|:---:|
| 1 | _____ | _____ |
| 2 | _____ | _____ |
| 3 | _____ | _____ |
| 4 | _____ | _____ |
| 5 | _____ | _____ |
| 6 | _____ | _____ |

▭ **C. *Why*** If you want to know the reason that a speaker chose a specific place, item, time, etc., ask *Why* and the specific word. Use the article if the word is a singular noun. Listen to these examples.

◢ **Example 1:**    A: I'm going to move to Arizona.
                B: Why Arizona?

◢ **Example 2:**    A: I'm going to buy a Ford.
                B: Why a Ford?

Now, complete these questions.

1. Why _____ ?
2. Why _____ ?
3. Why _____ ?
4. Why _____ ?
5. Why _____ ?
6. Why _____ ?
7. Why _____ ?
8. Why _____ ?
9. Why _____ ?
10. Why _____ ?

## INTERVIEWS

**In-Class Interview**   Interview a classmate about living in this state.

| | |
|---|---|
| 1. How do you like _____? <br> (state) | |
| 2. Why? (Why not?) | |
| 3. Is your family here? | |
| 4. How long have you lived in this state? | |
| 5. Do you ever think about moving? | |
| 6. Where would you move? | |
| 7. Why would you move there? | |

**Out-of-Class Interview**   Interview a friend, neighbor, or coworker about living in this state.

| | |
|---|---|
| 1. How do you like _____? <br> (state) | |
| 2. Why? (Why not?) | |
| 3. Is your family here? | |
| 4. How long have you lived in this state? | |
| 5. Do you ever think about moving? | |
| 6. Where would you move? | |
| 7. Why would you move there? | |

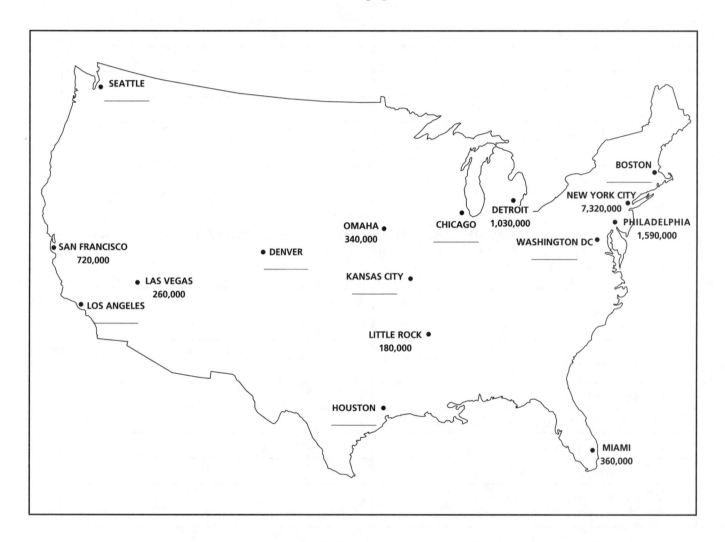

## FACE TO FACE

STUDENT A: The map below gives the population of several major cities. The population of other cities is blank. Ask Student B about the population of these cities. Write the missing information on the map. Then change roles. Student B will ask questions about the population of the cities on your map.

STUDENT B: Turn to page 135.

SEATTLE

BOSTON

NEW YORK CITY
7,320,000

DETROIT
1,030,000

CHICAGO

PHILADELPHIA
1,590,000

OMAHA
340,000

WASHINGTON DC

SAN FRANCISCO
720,000

DENVER

LAS VEGAS
260,000

KANSAS CITY

LOS ANGELES

LITTLE ROCK
180,000

HOUSTON

MIAMI
360,000

### *Helpful Language*

What's the population of ____(city)____ ?

Please repeat that number.

Excuse me?

Is that ____(number)____ ?

## INTERACTION

Each year, thousands of people move to the United States. In 1990, the United States admitted 1,500,000 immigrants. When people arrive, it is difficult to choose which town or city to live in.

A family from your country is going to immigrate to the United States. Should they consider the area you live in? Write three things you like about your area. Write three things you don't like. Sit in a small group and read your ideas. Other students can comment on your ideas and ask for your reasons. If you want, add two or three more ideas to your lists.

**I like**

_____

_____

_____

_____

_____

_____

**I don't like**

_____

_____

_____

_____

_____

_____

### *Helpful Language*

| | |
|---|---|
| I like _____ . | I don't like _____ . |
| How come? | How come? |
| You do? | You don't? |
| Why? | Why not? |

# JOBS FOR THE FUTURE

## COMPREHENSION

**A. Before You Listen**  Complete this information about your job or the job of someone you know. Several students should report their answers to the class. From the information, write two jobs for each list below. If a job has a good outlook, the number of workers and the number of jobs will be about the same. If a job has a poor outlook, there will be more workers than jobs. It will be difficult to find a job.

1.  Where do you work? _____

2.  What do you do? _____

3.  How is business?  _____ slow  _____ regular  _____ busy

4.  Is your company hiring new workers? _____

5.  Is your company laying off people? _____

   *Jobs with a Good Outlook*        *Jobs with a Poor Outlook*

   _____        _____

   _____        _____

**B. Key Words**  Discuss the new vocabulary, then complete the sentences below.

| | |
|---|---|
| **opening** | new position or job in a company |
| **(be) in demand** | to be a need for |
| **income** | salary; the money a person earns at a job |
| **rise** | to go up in number or price |
| **encourage** | to motivate; persuade |
| **concern** | worry |

1.  There is a lot of _____ about the increase in crime in our town.

2.  She can take a vacation trip this year because her _____ is higher.

3.  As the population gets older, nurses will be _____ .

4.  Our company has an _____ for a computer programmer.

5.  There is a _____ in the number of people who are retiring.

6.  New car prices _____ people to keep their old cars as long as possible.

**43**

**C. First Listening** You will hear about the job outlook for seven occupations. Listen and check the job outlook for each. After you listen, tell the class any other information you remember about the story.

| Occupation | Poor | Good | Excellent |
|---|---|---|---|
| 1. auto mechanic | _____ | _____ | _____ |
| 2. computer programmer | _____ | _____ | _____ |
| 3. mail carrier | _____ | _____ | _____ |
| 4. nurse | _____ | _____ | _____ |
| 5. travel agent | _____ | _____ | _____ |
| 6. guard | _____ | _____ | _____ |
| 7. teacher | _____ | _____ | _____ |

**D. Second Listening** Listen for the reason that there will be fewer or more jobs. Write the reason in three or four words.

| Occupation | Reason |
|---|---|
| 1. auto mechanic | _____ |
| 2. computer programmer | _____ |
| 3. mail carrier | _____ |
| 4. nurse | _____ |
| 5. travel agent | _____ |
| 6. guard | _____ |
| 7. teacher | _____ |

**E. Comprehension Questions** Listen and circle the correct answer.

1. a. the companies that are looking for workers
   b. job duties, salary, and outlook
   c. only those jobs that need a college education

2. a. A person will easily find a job as a mail carrier.
   b. A person will probably find a job as a mail carrier.
   c. A person probably won't find a job as a mail carrier.

3. a. There will be many jobs for computer programmers.
   b. People are buying computers for their homes.
   c. Prices of computers are going down.

4. a. People will keep their cars longer.
   b. Most cars only run well for the first year.
   c. Every family in this country has a car.

5.  a.  A college education is not required.
    b.  People have more money to travel.
    c.  It's easy to start a travel agency.

6.  a.  in the East
    b.  in the South
    c.  in the North

7.  a.  teacher
    b.  auto mechanic
    c.  security guard

# STRUCTURE

**A. Future Tense**  Listen to these sentences. Write the future verb you hear.

1.  _____will be_____          6.  _____
2.  _____          7.  _____
3.  _____          8.  _____
4.  _____          9.  _____
5.  _____         10.  _____

**B. Tense Contrast**  Listen to these sentences.  Decide if they are about now or the future. Circle *now* or *future*.

1.  now    future          6.  now    future
2.  now    future          7.  now    future
3.  now    future          8.  now    future
4.  now    future          9.  now    future
5.  now    future         10.  now    future

# PRONUNCIATION

**A. Stressed Syllables**  Listen and mark the stressed syllable.

> In a three-syllable word, one syllable is stressed. It is longer and louder.
>
> a. impórtant            c. expénsive
>
> b. góvernment          d. cómpany

| | | |
|---|---|---|
| 1. services | 6. computer | 11. openings |
| 2. United | 7. condition | 12. excellent |
| 3. deliver | 8. registered | 13. continue |
| 4. customer | 9. overseas | 14. vacation |
| 5. offices | 10. practical | 15. hospital |

**B. Numbers** This is a list of the average yearly salary for ten jobs. Listen and complete the information. You will hear each sentence twice.

| Job | Salary |
|---|---|
| 1. auto mechanic | $28,000 – $36,000 |
| 2. computer programmer | |
| 3. mail carrier | |
| 4. licensed practical nurse | |
| 5. registered nurse | |
| 6. travel agent | |
| 7. guard | |
| 8. police officer | |
| 9. elementary school teacher | |
| 10. secondary school teacher | |

# CONVERSATIONS

**A. Work** In each conversation, one person is speaking about his or her job. Check if the speaker is *working* or *not working*.

| Conversation | Working | Not Working |
|---|---|---|
| 1 | _____ | _____ |
| 2 | _____ | _____ |
| 3 | _____ | _____ |
| 4 | _____ | _____ |
| 5 | _____ | _____ |
| 6 | _____ | _____ |

**B. Worry** Listen to the conversations again. Two of the speakers are worried about their jobs. Circle the conversations in which the speakers are worried about their jobs.

Conversation 1            Conversation 4

Conversation 2            Conversation 5

Conversation 3            Conversation 6

▭  **C. Same or Different**  Read each sentence. Then, listen and decide if the meaning is the same or different. Circle *S* or *D*.

S   D   1.  Three workers quit.

S   D   2.  I might be the next one to leave.

S   D   3.  Where do you work?

S   D   4.  Why?

S   D   5.  You want to prepare for a new job.

S   D   6.  I will get some more information.

S   D   7.  Our salaries are high.

## INTERVIEWS

**In-Class Interview**  Interview a classmate who works.

| | |
|---|---|
| 1.  Where do you work? (Name of company) | |
| 2.  What do you do? | |
| 3.  How long have you worked there? | |
| 4.  Do you like your job? | |
| 5.  Do you work part time or full time? | |
| 6.  Is your company large or small? | |
| 7.  About how many people work there? | |
| 8.  Is your company busy? | |
| 9.  Are they hiring any new workers? | |
| 10.  What is the outlook for your job? | |

**Out-of-Class Interview**  Interview a friend or a neighbor who works.

| | |
|---|---|
| 1.  Where do you work? (Name of company) | |
| 2.  What do you do? | |
| 3.  How long have you worked there? | |
| 4.  Do you like your job? | |
| 5.  Do you work part time or full time? | |
| 6.  Is your company large or small? | |
| 7.  About how many people work there? | |
| 8.  Is your company busy? | |
| 9.  Are they hiring any new workers? | |
| 10.  What is the outlook for your job? | |

## 🎭 FACE TO FACE

STUDENT A: The incomplete chart below gives the average salary and outlook for 15 jobs. You have the information about half the jobs. Student B has the information about the other half. Ask and answer questions about the average salary and outlook for each job. Fill in the missing information.

STUDENT B: Turn to page 136.

| Job | Average Salary | Outlook |
|-----|----------------|---------|
| 1. accountant | _____ | _____ |
| 2. physical therapist | $38,000 | excellent |
| 3. telephone installer | _____ | _____ |
| 4. mechanical engineer | $53,000 | very good |
| 5. pharmacist | _____ | _____ |
| 6. social worker | $22,000 – $27,000 | very good |
| 7. family doctor | _____ | _____ |
| 8. jeweler | $25,000 – $30,000 | very good |
| 9. real estate agent | _____ | _____ |
| 10. funeral director | $21,000 – $28,000 | very good |
| 11. plumber | _____ | _____ |
| 12. electrical technician | $26,000 – $30,000 | fair |
| 13. carpenter | _____ | _____ |
| 14. dentist | $70,000 | good |
| 15. professional athlete | _____ | _____ |

### Helpful Language

What's the average salary for a/an __(job)__ ?

A/An __(job)__ earns / makes about $ _____ a year.

A/An __(job)__ earns / makes between $ _____ and
$ _____ a year.

What's the job outlook for a/an __(job)__ ?

# INTERACTION

Sit in a small group. You are planning for the future and are talking about the job market five years from now. Discuss the outlook for these four jobs. As a group, decide on the outlook and give your reasons. What other jobs are group members interested in? Write two more jobs and discuss their future.

1. Job outlook _____

Reason _____

_____

2. Job outlook _____

Reason _____

_____

3. Job outlook _____

Reason _____

_____

4. Job outlook _____

Reason _____

_____

- - - - - - - - - - - - - - - - - - - - - - - - - - - - - - - - - - - - - -

5. Job _____

Job outlook _____

Reason _____

_____

6. Job _____

Job outlook _____

Reason _____

_____

# Friends don't let friends drive drunk.

If your friend has had too much to drink, he doesn't have to drive.
Here are three ways to keep your friend alive . . .

## drive your friend home

## have your friend sleep over

U.S. Department of Transportation
**National Highway Traffic Safety
Administration**

## call a cab

| WEIGHT | | | | (DRINKS PER 2-HOUR PERIOD) | | | | | | | |
|---|---|---|---|---|---|---|---|---|---|---|---|
| 100 | 1 | 2 | 3 | 4 | 5 | 6 | 7 | 8 | 9 | 10 | 11 | 12 |
| 120 | 1 | 2 | 3 | 4 | 5 | 6 | 7 | 8 | 9 | 10 | 11 | 12 |
| 140 | 1 | 2 | 3 | 4 | 5 | 6 | 7 | 8 | 9 | 10 | 11 | 12 |
| 160 | 1 | 2 | 3 | 4 | 5 | 6 | 7 | 8 | 9 | 10 | 11 | 12 |
| 180 | 1 | 2 | 3 | 4 | 5 | 6 | 7 | 8 | 9 | 10 | 11 | 12 |
| 200 | 1 | 2 | 3 | 4 | 5 | 6 | 7 | 8 | 9 | 10 | 11 | 12 |
| 220 | 1 | 2 | 3 | 4 | 5 | 6 | 7 | 8 | 9 | 10 | 11 | 12 |
| 240 | 1 | 2 | 3 | 4 | 5 | 6 | 7 | 8 | 9 | 10 | 11 | 12 |

| BAC =<br>Blood<br>Alcohol<br>Content | YOU'RE<br>PLAYING<br>IT SAFE<br><br>Your blood<br>alcohol level<br>is below .05% | BE<br>CAREFUL<br><br>This amount<br>of alcohol<br>affects your<br>driving ability | DRIVING WHILE<br>INTOXICATED (DWI)<br>BAC = .10% & Above |
|---|---|---|---|

One drink =

One ½ oz. of 86 proof liquor

One 12 oz. can of beer

One 5 oz. glass of wine

# DRUNK DRIVER

## COMPREHENSION

**A. Before You Listen** Read and discuss the questions below.

Alcohol affects your ability to drive. Alcohol is not digested by the body. It passes through the stomach and into the bloodstream. A drink sometimes helps you to relax. But if you drink too much, it affects your reaction time, coordination, and balance.

1. On the chart on page 50, what is an acceptable blood-alcohol content (BAC) level? _____

   What is an illegal BAC level? _____

2. In some states, the BAC level is .15. What is the acceptable BAC level in your state? _____

3. Find your body weight on the chart. You are at a party for two hours. How many cans of beer could you drink and keep your blood-alcohol level at .05 or lower? _____

**B. Key Words** Discuss the new vocabulary, then complete the sentences below.

| | |
|---|---|
| **(on) watch** | a time to look for a specific person or thing |
| **prevent** | to stop; to keep something from happening |
| **injuries** | damage to a person's body |
| **weaving** | to move in and out, such as from left to right |
| **breath test** | a test in which a person blows air into a bag to show the level of alcohol in the blood |
| **issued a summons** | set a date a person must appear in court |
| **post bail** | to pay money to get a person out of jail, the person agrees to appear in court on a specific date |
| **offense** | a crime; an action which is against the law |
| **suspend** | to take away for a period of time |

1. The judge is going to _____ his license for six months.

2. The results of the _____ showed that she was drunk.

3. She had to _____ $500 _____ to get her brother out of jail.

4. The drunk driver is _____ in and out of traffic.

5. The police officer _____ for him to appear in court next week.

6. She received serious back and neck _____ in the accident.

7. We can _____ accidents by driving our friends home if they are drunk.

8. Drunk driving is a serious _____ .

9. The officers are on a special _____ , looking for drunk drivers.

**C. First Listening** Listen to this story about a drunk driver. As you listen, decide how many drinks you think Joe had at the party. After you listen, tell the class any other information you remember about the story.

**D. Second Listening** Read these sentences. Listen to the story again. Put the sentences in order from 1 to 8.

_____ a.  Joe decides to drive home.

_____ b.  Joe can't walk along a white line.

_____ c.  Joe is drinking at a family party.

_____ d.  The officer issues him a summons.

_____ e.  A police officer stops Joe.

_____ f.  The police officer arrests Joe and takes him to the police station.

_____ g.  Joe fails the breath test.

_____ h.  His sister posts $350 bail and drives him to her home.

**E. Comprehension Questions** Listen and circle the correct answer.

1.  a.  It's Officer Williams' first day on the job.
    b.  It's a holiday weekend.
    c.  It's a summer weekend.

2.  a.  40
    b.  400
    c.  4,000

3.  a.  to stop drinking
    b.  to drive home
    c.  to sleep over

4.  a.  at his sister's house
    b.  in the parking lot
    c.  on the main street

5.  a.  Joe is weaving in and out.
    b.  Joe is drinking in the car.
    c.  Joe went past the red light.

6.  a.  walk along a white line
    b.  pass the breath test
    c.  both a. and b.

7.  a.  He's going to take the bus.
    b.  He's going to rent a car.
    c.  He's going to drive.

**F. Penalties**  In Joe's state, there are strict penalties for driving while intoxicated. What are the penalties for first offense drunk driving in Joe's state?

1. _____
2. _____
3. _____
4. _____

# STRUCTURE

**A. Future Tense**  Listen to these sentences. Write the future verb you hear. In spoken English, *going to* sounds like *gonna*.

1. ___*is going to drive*___        6. _____
2. _____        7. _____
3. _____        8. _____
4. _____        9. _____
5. _____       10. _____

# PRONUNCIATION

**A. *His / Him***  Listen carefully and complete these sentences with *his* or *him*.

> We hear the ***h*** in *his* and *him* when it is the first word in a sentence.
>
> We often don't hear the ***h*** in *his* and *him* when it follows another word.
>
> > *His* often sounds like *ʰis*. — He's at ʰis sister's house.
> >
> > *Him* often sounds like *ʰim*. — She's talking to ʰim.

1. He's talking to _____ sister.
2. She's asking _____ to stay.
3. The officer arrested _____ .
4. They took _____ to the police station.
5. The officer is going to issue _____ a summons.
6. Joe's going to call _____ sister.
7. She's going to drive _____ to her house.
8. He can't drive _____ car home.
9. They're going to fine _____ $400.
10. He's going to lose _____ license.

**B. Stressed Words** Listen and complete these sentences with the stressed words.

> In speaking, the important words in a sentence are stressed.
> They are longer and louder. These are the content words
> (nouns, verbs, adjectives, and adverbs).

1. It's a _____ _____ .

2. _____ is at a _____ .

3. He's going to _____ .

4. She's _____ him to _____ .

5. I'm going to be _____ .

6. I'm going to _____ _____ .

7. The _____ is going to _____ him to

   the _____ _____ .

8. His _____ is going to _____ him to

   _____ _____ .

9. The _____ is going to _____ his

   _____ .

10. He was _____ to _____ and

    _____ .

# CONVERSATIONS

**A. Match** These cases are being heard in municipal court. In each, the judge is speaking with a person who received a ticket for a motor vehicle violation. Write the number of the conversation on the correct picture.

1. _____

2. _____

3. _____

4. _____    5. _____    6. _____

_____    _____    _____

🔲 **B. Charges and Fines**  Listen again. On the first line under each picture, write the charge. On the second line, write the total amount of the fine and court costs.

🔲 **C. Question Intonation**  This judge asked several questions. At times, he used a question with question intonation. At other times, he used a statement with question intonation. Listen to the intonation of these sentences. Put a period if you hear a statement. Put a question mark if you hear a question.

▲ **Examples:**

**There was an accident.**    statement

**Was there an accident?**    question

**There was an accident?**    question

1.  There was an accident **?**____

2.  You were driving 40 miles per hour ____

3.  No emergency vehicles came ____

4.  They weren't in the vehicle ____

5.  The fine is $40 ____

6.  This summons was issued on March 10th ____

7.  And the same problem with the registration ____

8.  This is a very serious offense ____

9.  You understand the charge ____

10. You have an explanation ____

# INTERVIEWS

**In-Class Interview**  In small groups, interview a student who received a ticket.

| | |
|---|---|
| 1.  Did you ever receive a ticket? | |
| 2.  What was the ticket for? | |
| 3.  Did you have to go to court? | |
| 4.  How much was the fine? | |
| 5.  Was there any other penalty? | |
| 6.  Was your license suspended? | |
| 7.  Did your insurance go up? | |

**Out-of-Class Interview**  Interview a friend, neighbor, or coworker who received a ticket.

| | |
|---|---|
| 1.  Did you ever receive a ticket? | |
| 2.  What was the ticket for? | |
| 3.  Did you have to go to court? | |
| 4.  How much was the fine? | |
| 5.  Was there any other penalty? | |
| 6.  Was your license suspended? | |
| 7.  Did your insurance go up? | |

# FACE TO FACE

STUDENT A:  You and Student B both have pictures of an accident scene. There are seven differences in your pictures. Talk about your pictures. Try to find the differences. Do not look at your partner's picture.

STUDENT B:  Turn to page 137.

## INTERACTION

Drunk driving is one of the most serious motor vehicle violations in this country. If there is an accident and a passenger or another driver is hurt, drunk driving can also be a criminal offense. If you serve alcohol at a party and a guest drives home after drinking too much, you are partly responsible if there is an accident.

Sit in a small group of three or four students. What would you do in each of the following situations? Write your answer after you discuss each situation. When you finish, compare the responses of two or three groups.

1.  You give a party. A friend had four or five drinks that evening. She says she can drive herself home.

    _____

2.  You are at a party with Jack. He had five cans of beer in two hours. He seems fine, but he is talking a little loud. It's time to leave. You ask for the car keys so that you can drive. Jack becomes angry and won't give them to you.

    _____

3.  You were at a party and had three drinks. You are driving home slowly and carefully. A police officer stops you and asks you to take a breath test. You don't know if you will pass it.

    _____

4.  You are driving home at 3 A.M. The car in front of you is going very slowly, weaving in and out.

    _____

5.  Your teenage daughter borrowed the car and went to a party. You receive a call at 12:00 A.M. The police stopped her for drunk driving and she's at the police station.

    _____

# A PROFESSIONAL

## COMPREHENSION

**A. Before You Listen** One in six Americans is worried about a burglary. You can expect to have your home robbed twice in your lifetime. These are some of the most common forms of security. Do you use any of the following? Circle any of the following that you use.

1. a dead-bolt lock
2. an automatic timer
3. a peephole in the door
4. an alarm system decal
5. special window locks

6. a gun
7. a dog
8. a chainlock
9. an unlisted phone number
10. a motion detector light

**B. Key Words** Discuss the new vocabulary, then complete the sentences below.

| | |
|---|---|
| **thief** | a person who steals |
| **typical** | regular; the same as usual |
| **briefcase** | a bag for carrying business papers |
| **screwdriver** | a tool to put screws in and take them out |
| **climbed** | to go up or down, often using the hands and feet |
| **necklace** | a piece of jewelry that is worn around the neck |

1. She wore a beautiful emerald _____ with her dress.
2. The _____ took their TV and their stereo.
3. A business man or woman carries a _____ to work.
4. The thief _____ in the window.
5. The thief used a _____ to open the window.
6. On a _____ day, he leaves his house at 8:00.

**C. First Listening** Look at the picture on page 58 and listen to this story about a professional thief. As you listen, decide why Richard chose this house to rob. After you listen, tell the class any other information you remember about the story.

**D. Second Listening** Listen to the story again. Circle the items that Richard stole.

**E. Comprehension Questions** Listen and circle the correct answer.

1. a. because he's a professional
   b. because he didn't want anyone to look at him
   c. because he works hard

2. a. he entered the house
   b. he stood behind a tree
   c. he walked around the block again

3. a. because it was nighttime
   b. because he wore a business suit
   c. because he stood behind a tree

4. a. It was too big.
   b. It was too heavy.
   c. It was too old.

5. a. five minutes
   b. fifteen minutes
   c. one hour

6. a. a camera
   b. a stereo
   c. a computer

7. a. a sunny day
   b. a rainy day
   c. a snowy day

# STRUCTURE

**A. Past Tense** Listen to these sentences. Write the past tense verb you hear.

1. _____dressed_____    6. _____

2. _____    7. _____

3. _____    8. _____

4. _____    9. _____

5. _____    10. _____

**B. Tense Contrast** Listen to these sentences. Decide the tense of the verb. Circle *present*, *past*, or *future*.

1. present    past    future    6. present    past    future

2. present    past    future    7. present    past    future

3. present    past    future    8. present    past    future

4. present    past    future    9. present    past    future

5. present    past    future    10. present    past    future

# PRONUNCIATION

**A. *-ed* Endings** Say each of these past tense verbs to yourself. Decide if it has one or two syllables. Then, listen to the pronunciation of each verb. Write the number of syllables you hear.

| | Before you listen | After you listen | | | Before you listen | After you listen |
|---|---|---|---|---|---|---|
| 1. parked | ____ | ____ | 8. waited | ____ | ____ | |
| 2. wanted | ____ | ____ | 9. walked | ____ | ____ | |
| 3. dressed | ____ | ____ | 10. started | ____ | ____ | |
| 4. worked | ____ | ____ | 11. robbed | ____ | ____ | |
| 5. needed | ____ | ____ | 12. carried | ____ | ____ | |
| 6. said | ____ | ____ | 13. hated | ____ | ____ | |
| 7. climbed | ____ | ____ | 14. arrived | ____ | ____ | |

**B. Linking with -ed** Listen carefully and complete these sentences with the missing words. Mark the linking sounds.

> When a final **-ed** is followed by a vowel, the sounds are linked.
> The **-d** sounds like part of the next word.
> He watche**d a** woman leave the house.

1. He _____ parked on _____ Main Street.
2. He _____ _____ a business suit.
3. He _____ _____ the block.
4. He _____ _____ color TV.
5. He _____ _____ the morning.
6. He _____ _____ briefcase.
7. He _____ _____ window.
8. He _____ _____ .
9. He _____ _____ 8:15.
10. He _____ _____ house every day.

**C. Stressed Words** Listen and complete these sentences with the stressed words.

> In speaking, the important words in a sentence are stressed.
> They are longer and louder. These are the content words
> (nouns, verbs, adjectives, and adverbs).
> He **stóle** a **ríng** and a **nécklace.**

1. _____ _____ _____ .
2. His _____ is _____ .
3. He _____ to a _____ about _____ _____ from
   his _____ .
4. He _____ his _____ in a _____ _____ .
5. A _____ was _____ his _____ .
6. _____ _____ to the _____ of the
   _____ .
7. He _____ a _____ out of his _____ .
8. He _____ the _____ and _____ in.
9. He _____ through the _____ in the _____
   _____ .
10. He _____ $_____ in _____ .

# CONVERSATIONS

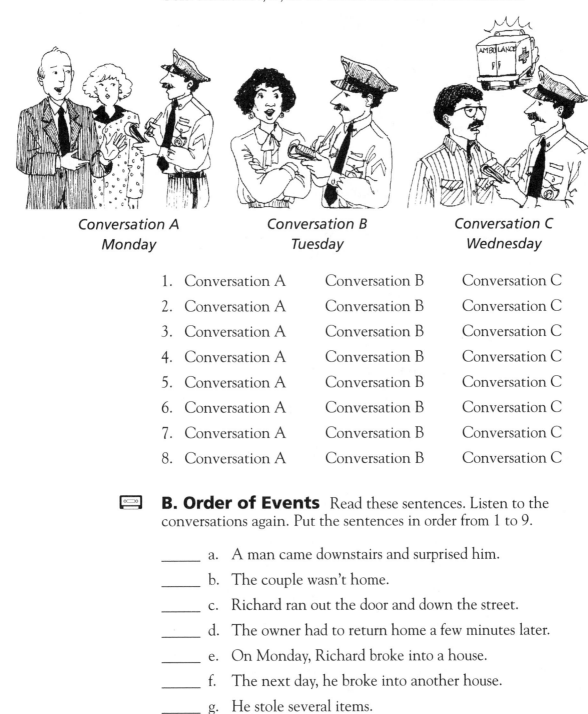

**A. Three Robberies** Look at the pictures and listen to these three conversations between a police officer and three families that Richard robbed. Then, listen to sentences from the conversations. Do they refer to Conversation A, B, or C? Circle the correct conversation.

*Conversation A*
*Monday*

*Conversation B*
*Tuesday*

*Conversation C*
*Wednesday*

| | | | |
|---|---|---|---|
| 1. | Conversation A | Conversation B | Conversation C |
| 2. | Conversation A | Conversation B | Conversation C |
| 3. | Conversation A | Conversation B | Conversation C |
| 4. | Conversation A | Conversation B | Conversation C |
| 5. | Conversation A | Conversation B | Conversation C |
| 6. | Conversation A | Conversation B | Conversation C |
| 7. | Conversation A | Conversation B | Conversation C |
| 8. | Conversation A | Conversation B | Conversation C |

**B. Order of Events** Read these sentences. Listen to the conversations again. Put the sentences in order from 1 to 9.

_____ a.  A man came downstairs and surprised him.

_____ b.  The couple wasn't home.

_____ c.  Richard ran out the door and down the street.

_____ d.  The owner had to return home a few minutes later.

_____ e.  On Monday, Richard broke into a house.

_____ f.  The next day, he broke into another house.

_____ g.  He stole several items.

_____ h.  Richard broke into a third house.

_____ i.  Richard ran out the door, and he fell down the front steps.

**C. Same or Different** Read each sentence. Then, listen and decide if the meaning is the same or different. Circle *S* or *D*.

S  D  1. My diamond ring is here.

S  D  2. Which direction did he go?

S  D  3. Did you see the license plate number?

S  D  4. Is he good looking?

S  D  5. He didn't expect to see me.

S  D  6. He thought no one was home.

S  D  7. I agree!

S  D  8. He broke twenty windows.

**D. Questions with *Did*** Listen to these questions about the robberies. Complete them with *Did he*, *Did she*, or *Did you*.

**Examples:**

**Did he climb in the window?**

**Did she run after the thief?**

**Did you get the license plate number?**

1. _____ _____ take anything?

2. _____ _____ get his license?

3. _____ _____ surprise him?

4. _____ _____ have a gun?

5. _____ _____ break the window?

6. _____ _____ get a good look at him?

7. _____ _____ call the police?

8. _____ _____ hear something downstairs?

9. _____ _____ run after him?

10. _____ _____ say anything to you?

# INTERVIEWS

**In-Class Interview**  Sit in a small group. Interview a student who was robbed or who knows about a robbery.

| | |
|---|---|
| 1. Did anyone ever rob you (or someone you know)? | |
| 2. Where were you living? | |
| 3. How did the thief get in the house? | |
| 4. What time of day was it? | |
| 5. Was anyone home? | |
| 6. What did the thief take? | |
| 7. Did you see the thief? | |
| 8. Did you call the police? | |
| 9. Did they ever catch the thief? | |

**Out-of-Class Interview**  Interview a friend, neighbor, or coworker.

| | |
|---|---|
| 1. Did anyone ever rob you (or someone you know)? | |
| 2. Where were you living? | |
| 3. How did the thief get in the house? | |
| 4. What time of day was it? | |
| 5. Was anyone home? | |
| 6. What did the thief take? | |
| 7. Did you see the thief? | |
| 8. Did you call the police? | |
| 9. Did they ever catch the thief? | |

# 👥 FACE TO FACE

STUDENT A: Yesterday a thief broke into Kim's apartment. You have a picture of Kim's apartment before it was robbed. Student B has a picture of Kim's apartment after it was robbed. Talk together about the contents of the apartment and decide what items were taken. Cross out the eight items that the thief stole. Do not look at Student B's picture.

STUDENT B: Turn to page 138.

## *Helpful Language*

Did the thief take the _____?

Is there still a _____ (on the counter)?

# INTERACTION

Last night when Lisa was sleeping, a thief broke into her apartment.

In a small group, put the pictures in order from 1 to 6. Talk about what happened. Then, write the story of the robbery.

_____

_____

_____

_____

_____

_____

_____

_____

_____

_____

# THE LOTTERY

## COMPREHENSION

### A. Before You Listen

Write your favorite number. _____

Explain why it is your favorite number.

Circle the numbers below that are lucky numbers in your country. Cross out the unlucky numbers. Explain your reasons.

| 1  | 2  | 3  | 4  | 5  | 6  | 7  | 8  | 9  | 10 |
| 11 | 12 | 13 | 14 | 15 | 16 | 17 | 18 | 19 | 20 |
| 21 | 22 | 23 | 24 | 25 | 26 | 27 | 28 | 29 | 30 |

### B. Key Words  Discuss the new vocabulary, then complete the sentences below.

| total | all; the complete amount |
| fault | responsibility for a mistake |
| opportunity | chance; a good time to do or try something |
| bored | a feeling of not being interested |
| immediately | right now, without delay |
| security | a feeling of safety, of not being worried |

1. My father retired and he doesn't know what to do with his time. He's _____ .

2. Money in the bank brings _____ . You know that if you need it, it's there.

3. She won a _____ of $50,000.

4. If I don't do well in school, it's my _____ .

5. When she saw that she had a winning lottery ticket, she _____ called her parents.

6. He has the _____ to travel to Japan this summer.

**C. First Listening** Look at the picture on page 68 and listen to this story about four lottery winners. As you listen, write down the amount of money that each person won in the lottery. After you listen, tell the class any other information you remember about the story.

1. Lisa K.    _____

2. Mark L.    _____

3. Mabel S.    _____

4. Jack B.    _____

**D. Second Listening** Listen to the story again. As you listen, write what these people were doing before they won the lottery. Then, write what they are doing now.

| Name | Before | Now |
|------|--------|-----|
| 1. Lisa K. | | |
| 2. Mark L. | | |
| 3. Mabel S. | | |
| 4. Jack B. | | |

**E. Comprehension Questions** Listen and circle the correct answer.

1. a. more than a thousand

   b. more than a hundred thousand

   c. more than a million

2. a. $1,000,000

   b. $50,000

   c. $25,000 to $40,000

3. a. They bought new cars.

   b. They quit their jobs.

   c. They went back to school.

4. a. She wants to have a lot of money.

   b. She wants to become an artist.

   c. She wants to quit her job.

5.  a.  He wants to sell cars again.

   b.  He's bored.

   c.  He doesn't have enough time for his family.

6.  a.  She's going to spend it more carefully.

   b.  She's going to buy a car.

   c.  She's going to save it.

7.  a.  Happiness

   b.  Good friends

   c.  Security

# STRUCTURE

**A. Past Irregular Verbs**  Listen to these sentences. Write the verb you hear.

1.  _____bought_____          6.  _____

2.  _____          7.  _____

3.  _____          8.  _____

4.  _____          9.  _____

5.  _____         10.  _____

**B. Negatives**  Listen to these sentences. Circle the negative verb you hear.

1.  a. don't quit          b. doesn't quit          c. didn't quit

2.  a. don't worry         b. doesn't worry         c. didn't worry

3.  a. don't enjoy         b. doesn't enjoy         c. didn't enjoy

4.  a. don't become        b. doesn't become        c. didn't become

5.  a. don't have          b. doesn't have          c. didn't have

6.  a. don't know          b. doesn't know          c. didn't know

7.  a. don't have          b. doesn't have          c. didn't have

8.  a. don't want          b. doesn't want          c. didn't want

9.  a. don't spend         b. doesn't spend         c. didn't spend

10.  a. don't have          b. doesn't have          c. didn't have

# PRONUNCIATION

**A. Linking with *A / An*** Complete these sentences with the missing words. Mark the linking sounds.

> When a final consonant is followed by *a* or *an,* the sounds are linked.
>
> *A* or *an* sounds like part of the word before.
>
> He **won a** million dollars.

1. _____ _____ person _____ _____ million dollars, he must pay taxes.
2. He doesn't _____ _____ check for the total amount.
3. She _____ _____ cashier.
4. She wants to _____ _____ artist.
5. Mark _____ _____ car salesman.
6. He worked seven _____ _____ week.
7. She _____ _____ million dollars.
8. She _____ _____ new car.
9. He teaches _____ _____ high school.
10. Money _____ _____ person opportunities.

**B. *Did he / Does he*** *Did he* and *Does he* can sound similar. Listen and complete these questions with *Did he* or *Does he*.

> We often do not hear the sound of the *h* after *did* or *does.*
>
> Did he like his job? — Did he like his job?
> Does he like his job? — Does he like his job?

1. _____ _____ buy a ticket?
2. _____ _____ work now?
3. _____ _____ like his job?
4. _____ _____ work at home now?
5. _____ _____ know what he wants to do?
6. _____ _____ win two million dollars?
7. _____ _____ quit his job?
8. _____ _____ still teach English?
9. _____ _____ have a new car?
10. _____ _____ worry about money?

# CONVERSATIONS

**A. Match** Listen to each person talk about lottery tickets. Listen for how many lottery tickets each person buys a week. Complete the information below.

| Conversation | Number of Tickets |
|---|---|
| 1 | _____ |
| 2 | _____ |
| 3 | _____ |
| 4 | _____ |
| 5 | _____ |
| 6 | _____ |
| 7 | _____ |

**B. Which Conversation?** Read the statements below. Each one talks about a person in one of the conversations. Listen to each conversation again. Write the number of the correct conversation.

_____ a.  This person used to buy lottery tickets, but he doesn't anymore.

_____ b.  This person's relative won the lottery.

_____ c.  This person always plays his lucky numbers.

_____ d.  This person only buys tickets when the jackpot is high.

_____ e.  This person would like to stop buying tickets, but he can't.

_____ f.  This person is sure that she's going to win the lottery.

_____ g.  This person won some money.

**C. Same or Different** Read each sentence. Then, listen and decide if the meaning is the same or different. Circle *S* or *D*.

S   D   1.  I don't win any money.

S   D   2.  I'm not going to buy any more tickets.

S   D   3.  They need money for their other expenses.

S   D   4.  I still buy tickets.

S   D   5.  I'm going to buy another ticket.

S   D   6.  I'm going to win the lottery.

S   D   7.  I stop at the store for tickets when I'm driving home.

# INTERVIEWS

**In-Class Interview**  Interview a student in your class.

| | |
|---|---|
| 1.  Are you a lucky person? | |
| 2.  Why or why not? | |
| 3.  What's your lucky number? | |
| 4.  Does this state have a state lottery? | |
| 5.  Do you ever buy lottery tickets? | |
| 6.  How many a week? | |
| 7.  Did you ever win any money? | |
| 8.  Did you ever lose any money? | |
| 9.  What would you do if you won the lottery? | |

**Out-of-Class Interview**  Interview a friend, neighbor, or coworker.

| | |
|---|---|
| 1.  Are you a lucky person? | |
| 2.  Why or why not? | |
| 3.  What's your lucky number? | |
| 4.  Does this state have a state lottery? | |
| 5.  Do you ever buy lottery tickets? | |
| 6.  How many a week? | |
| 7.  Did you ever win any money? | |
| 8.  Did you ever lose any money? | |
| 9.  What would you do if you won the lottery? | |

# 👥 FACE TO FACE

STUDENT A: This picture shows twelve people who won the lottery. You and Student B have information about how six different people spent their winnings. Ask and answer questions about these winners. Draw a line from each person to the action.

STUDENT B: Turn to page 139.

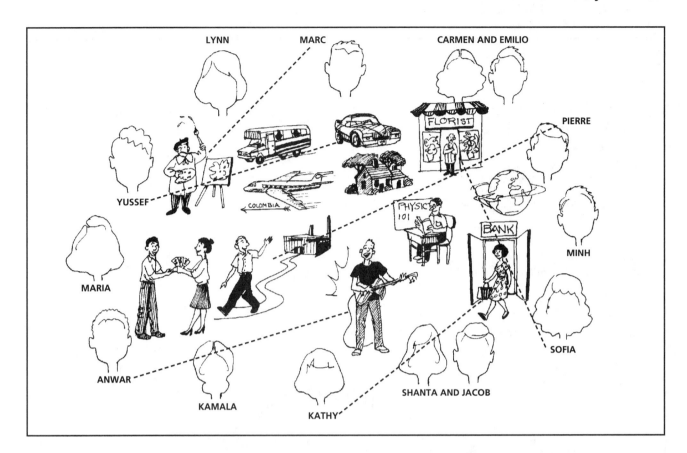

### *Helpful language*

What did _____ do with the money?

## INTERACTION

Sit with a partner. This is a Pick-6 lottery form. If a person picks the correct six numbers between 1 and 49, the prize is one million dollars or more. Talk together and pick six numbers between 1 and 49. Circle them on the form. Tell another group your numbers. Explain how you chose your numbers.

| PICK 6 LOTTERY | | | | | | |
|---|---|---|---|---|---|---|
| 1 | 2 | 3 | 4 | 5 | 6 | 7 |
| 8 | 9 | 10 | 11 | 12 | 13 | 14 |
| 15 | 16 | 17 | 18 | 19 | 20 | 21 |
| 22 | 23 | 24 | 25 | 26 | 27 | 28 |
| 29 | 30 | 31 | 32 | 33 | 34 | 35 |
| 36 | 37 | 38 | 39 | 40 | 41 | 42 |
| 43 | 44 | 45 | 46 | 47 | 48 | 49 |

### *Helpful Language*

I like that number, too.          I don't like that number.

What do you think?          No, that's an unlucky number.

How about number _____?

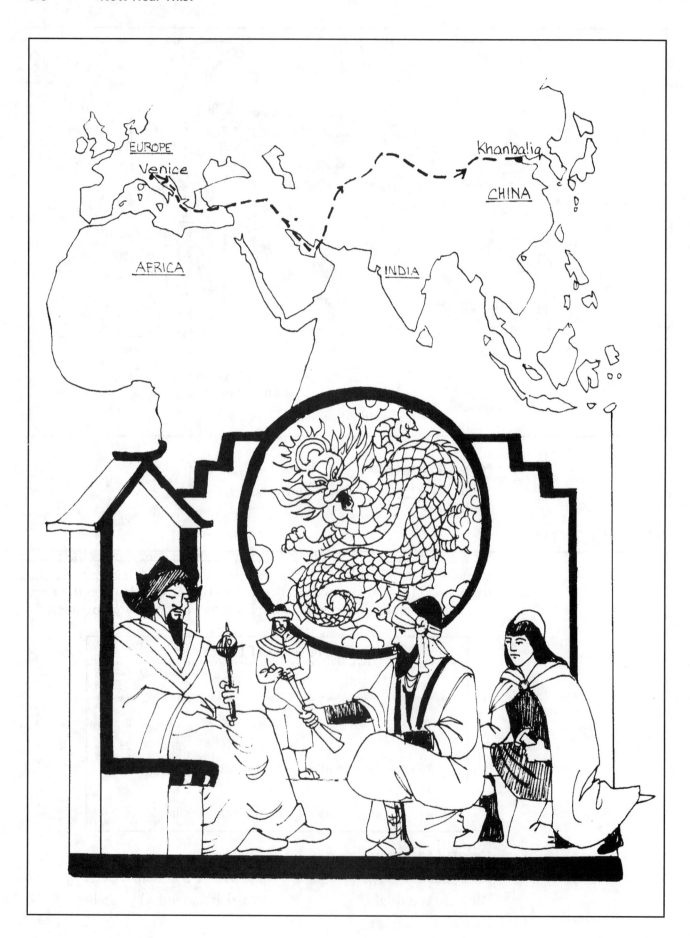

# MARCO POLO

## COMPREHENSION

**A. Before You Listen** Match these famous travelers with the year of their accomplishments. (Check your answers on page 129.)

_____ 1. Charles Lindbergh flies from New York to Paris.

_____ 2. Leif Ericson lands in North America.

_____ 3. Yuri Gagarin travels in space.

_____ 4. Marco Polo visits China.

_____ 5. Neil Armstrong walks on the moon.

_____ 6. Ferdinand Magellan sails around the world.

a. 1000

b. 1275

c. 1521

d. 1927

e. 1961

f. 1969

**B. Key Words** Discuss the new vocabulary, then complete the sentences below.

| | |
|---|---|
| **travelers** | people who visit different places or countries |
| **palace** | the large, beautiful home of a king or emperor |
| **emperor** | the ruler of a country |
| **amazed** | surprised |
| **advanced** | far in front in progress or development |
| **dig – dug** | to make a hole in the ground, often with a shovel |
| **paved** | to cover a road with stones or cement |
| **bark** | the outer covering of a tree |

1. A long time ago, people used the _____ of trees for paper.

2. Kublai Khan was the powerful _____ of China in 1275.

3. The highways of China were more _____ than those in Europe.

4. The emperor lived in a _____ on top of a mountain.

5. People _____ black stones out of the ground.

6. Marco Polo was one of the first European _____ to China.

7. Marco Polo was _____ to see a strange animal along the rivers.

8. The Chinese _____ their highways with stones.

**C. First Listening** Listen to this story about Marco Polo. The story describes five things in China that amazed people because they were so different from Italy at that time. As you listen, write the names of these five things. Tell the class any other information you remember about the story.

1. _____

2. _____

3. _____

4. _____

5. _____

**D. Second Listening** Read these sentences. Then, listen to the story again. Decide which country each sentence describes in the year 1275. Write C for *China* or I for *Italy*.

1. _____ People bathed at least three times a week.

2. _____ People bathed about once a week.

3. _____ People traveled on paved roads.

4. _____ People traveled on dirt roads.

5. _____ People heated their homes with wood.

6. _____ People heated their homes with coal.

7. _____ People used gold and silver to buy and sell things.

8. _____ People used paper money or gold and silver to buy and sell things.

9. _____ There were crocodiles in the southern areas of this country.

10. _____ There were no crocodiles in this country.

**E. Comprehension Questions** Listen and circle the correct answer.

1.  a.  Italy
    b.  Europe
    c.  China

2.  a.  Yes, he traveled alone.
    b.  No, he traveled with his father and uncle.
    c.  No, he traveled with a group of Europeans.

3.  a.  for three years
    b.  for 20 years
    c.  in 1275

4.  a.  by coal
    b.  by wood
    c.  by electricity

5.  a.  because Europe had paved roads, too
    b.  because Europe had dirt roads
    c.  because Europe didn't need paved roads

6.  a.  elephants
    b.  tigers
    c.  crocodiles

7.  a.  Yes, everyone did.
    b.  No, no one did.
    c.  Some people did and some people didn't.

# STRUCTURE

**A. Past Irregular Tense** Listen to these sentences. Write the past tense verb you hear.

1.  _____left_____          6.  _____

2.  _____        7.  _____

3.  _____        8.  _____

4.  _____        9.  _____

5.  _____       10.  _____

**B. *One of the* + adjective**  Listen and complete these sentences with *one of the* and the adjective.

> In *one of the,* the words are linked. We usually don't hear the **f** in *of.*
>
> Kublai Khan was **one of the** most powerful emperors of China.

1. Marco Polo was _____ ___ _____ _____ _____ travelers of all times.
2. He was _____ ___ _____ _____ Europeans to visit China.
3. China was _____ ___ _____ _____ _____ countries in the world.
4. Kublai Khan was _____ ___ _____ _____ emperors of China.
5. *Description of the World* became _____ ___ _____ _____ _____ books in Europe.
6. China had _____ ___ _____ _____ _____ highway systems in the world.
7. It was _____ ___ _____ _____ countries to use paper money.
8. The crocodile was _____ ___ _____ _____ animals that Marco Polo ever saw.

# PRONUNCIATION

**A. *Was / Were***  Listen to these sentences. Circle *was* or *were.*

1. was    were
2. was    were
3. was    were
4. was    were
5. was    were
6. was    were
7. was    were
8. was    were
9. was    were
10. was    were

**B. Linking with -ed** Listen carefully and complete these sentences with the missing words. Mark the linking sounds.

> When a final **-ed** is followed by a vowel, the sounds are linked.
> The **-d** sounds like part of the next word.
> People were surprise**d at** his stories.

1. Marco Polo and his father _____ _____ China for 20 years.

2. They _____ _____ the palace of the emperor.

3. They _____ _____ China for many years.

4. The Chinese _____ _____ least three times a week.

5. They _____ _____ with the royal seal.

6. Marco Polo _____ _____ the strange animal in the river.

7. The Polos _____ _____ by horse and camel.

8. Marco Polo _____ _____ his travels with a friend.

9. Some people _____ _____ his stories.

10. Everyone was _____ _____ his stories of China.

## CONVERSATIONS

**A. Match** In 1275, Marco Polo was amazed by the modern advances in China. In the world today, it is difficult to follow all the new advances in technology. Listen to each conversation. Number the correct picture.

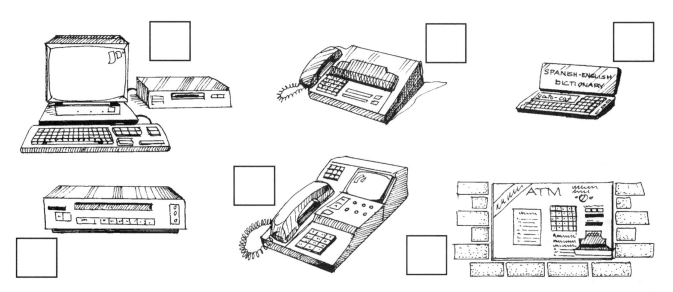

**B. Meaning** Listen to each sentence. Circle the letter of the sentence with the same meaning.

1. a. How do you do it?
   b. Why?

2. a. Is there a problem with the machine?
   b. Did you buy the wrong machine?

3. a. I don't know how to use most electronic equipment.
   b. This equipment is no good.

4. a. My father is thinking about buying a video phone.
   b. My father is definitely going to buy a video phone.

5. a. I like the idea.
   b. I don't like the idea.

6. a. I only use the mail.
   b. I don't use the mail anymore.

7. a. I do, too.
   b. I don't, either.

8. a. I go to the bank one or two times a week.
   b. In the past, I went to the bank one or two times a week.

**C. Conversation Fillers (*Well / I mean / Like / You know*)**
In informal conversation, people often use conversation fillers. Some people, especially young people, use fillers in almost every sentence. These words have no meaning. They give the speaker time to pause and then continue the conversation. Common fillers are *Well, I mean, like,* and *you know*. Listen to these sentences and circle the fillers you hear.

1. Well    I mean    like    you know
2. Well    I mean    like    you know
3. Well    I mean    like    you know
4. Well    I mean    like    you know
5. Well    I mean    like    you know
6. Well    I mean    like    you know
7. Well    I mean    like    you know
8. Well    I mean    like    you know
9. Well    I mean    like    you know
10. Well    I mean    like    you know

# INTERVIEWS

**In-Class Interview**   Interview another student about each electronic or computer item below. Check the appropriate boxes.

*Do you own a _____?*

*Do you plan to buy one?*

| Item | Owns one | Plans to buy one | Doesn't plan to buy one |
|---|---|---|---|
| 1.  computer | | | |
| 2.  laptop computer | | | |
| 3.  video phone | | | |
| 4.  CD player | | | |
| 5.  fax machine | | | |
| 6.  cellular phone | | | |
| 7.  personal pager | | | |

**Out-of-Class Interview**   Interview a friend, neighbor, or coworker about each electronic or computer item below. Check the appropriate boxes.

*Do you own a _____?*

*Do you plan to buy one?*

| Item | Owns one | Plans to buy one | Doesn't plan to buy one |
|---|---|---|---|
| 1.  computer | | | |
| 2.  laptop computer | | | |
| 3.  video phone | | | |
| 4.  CD player | | | |
| 5.  fax machine | | | |
| 6.  cellular phone | | | |
| 7.  personal pager | | | |

## 👥 FACE TO FACE

STUDENT A: You have a picture of a computer with six parts labeled:

1. monitor
2. on/off switch
3. keyboard
4. keyboard cable
5. mouse
6. mouse pad

Student B has the same computer with six different parts labeled. Talk about the computer, naming and describing the parts. Try to label all the parts of the computer.

STUDENT B: Turn to page 140.

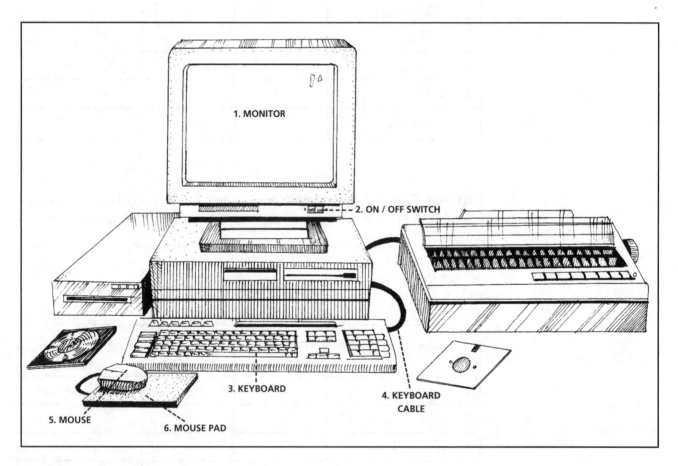

**1. MONITOR**

**2. ON / OFF SWITCH**

**3. KEYBOARD**

**4. KEYBOARD CABLE**

**5. MOUSE**

**6. MOUSE PAD**

### *Helpful Language*

Number 1 is the monitor.

Where's the monitor?

It's on (under, next to, in front of) the computer.

What's a monitor?

It's like a TV screen. you see words or pictures on it.

How do you spell monitor?

# INTERACTION

Sit in a group of three students. The electronic age is here. A few years ago, most households had a stereo and a TV. Now, electronic stores offer hundreds of items. Write the names of five electronic items you have bought in the last five years.

1. _____

2. _____

3. _____

4. _____

5. _____

In the box, draw a picture of one of the items on your list. Your group will ask you the questions below about the item you drew.

1. What brand (kind) did you buy?

2. Where did you buy it?

3. What do you use it for?

4. How often do you use it?

5. Is it easy to use?

6. Does it have a warranty?

7. Do you ever have problems with it?

8. What's the price range for this item?

9. If I buy this item, what features are important?

# CAN I BORROW A DOLLAR? 11

## COMPREHENSION

**A. Before You Listen** Did anyone ever borrow one of these items from you? Who borrowed it? When did the person return it?

_____ your car

_____ money

_____ a tape or a CD

_____ clothes, for example, a dress to wear to a party

_____ your dictionary

_____ a tool, such as a power saw or a drill

**B. Key Words** Discuss the new vocabulary, then complete the sentences below.

| | |
|---|---|
| **several** | more than two, but not many |
| **break** | a rest time at work or school |
| **bill** | a paper that tells the items bought and their prices |
| **pay back** | to return money that a person borrowed |
| **wallet** | a small case for keeping money, credit cards, etc. |
| **(be) broke** | to not have any money |

1.  Can I borrow five dollars? I'll _____ you _____ tomorrow.

2.  Those people are renting _____ videos.

3.  On their _____ , the workers usually sit and talk.

4.  The _____ for lunch was ten dollars.

5.  I don't have any money because I forgot my _____ .

6.  I can't lend you any money. I'm _____ .

**C. First Listening** Steve is always borrowing money from Hoang. Listen to the story and check the items that Steve needed money for. After you listen, tell the class any other information you remember about the story.

_____ 1. his books      _____ 5. lunch

_____ 2. a video      _____ 6. gas

_____ 3. a soda      _____ 7. a present for his Mom

_____ 4. a wallet      _____ 8. a haircut

**D. Figure It Out** Listen again. Figure out how much money Steve borrowed from Hoang.

_____

**E. Listen and Decide** Listen to Steve's requests. Circle Hoang's response.

1. a. Sure. / No problem.    b. Well, okay.    c. Sorry.
2. a. Sure. / No problem.    b. Well, okay.    c. Sorry.
3. a. Sure. / No problem.    b. Well, okay.    c. Sorry.
4. a. Sure. / No problem.    b. Well, okay.    c. Sorry.

# STRUCTURE

**A. Requests** Listen to these requests. Each starts with _Can I, Can you, Could I,_ or _Could you_. Write the sentences you hear. You will hear each sentence twice.

1. <u>Can I borrow $10?</u>
2. _____
3. _____
4. _____
5. _____
6. _____
7. _____

**B. Tense Contrast** Listen to these sentences. Decide the tense of the verb. Circle _present, past,_ or _future_.

1. present   past   future     6. present   past   future
2. present   past   future     7. present   past   future
3. present   past   future     8. present   past   future
4. present   past   future     9. present   past   future
5. present   past   future    10. present   past   future

# PRONUNCIATION

**A. *To*** Listen to these common reductions for *to*. Then complete the sentences.

| | |
|---|---|
| *want to — wanna* | *have to — hafta* |
| *need to — needta* or *needa* | *has to — hasta* |
| *going to — gonna* | |

1.  I _____ \_\_\_\_\_ get a haircut.

2.  I _____ \_\_\_\_\_ buy some gas.

3.  He _____ \_\_\_\_\_ earn money for college.

4.  I _____ \_\_\_\_\_ work part time.

5.  I _____ \_\_\_\_\_ get a soda.

6.  I _____ \_\_\_\_\_ make a phone call.

7.  He _____ \_\_\_\_\_ pay for his clothes.

8.  I'm _____ \_\_\_\_\_ borrow some money.

9.  I _____ \_\_\_\_\_ take a break.

10. He's _____ \_\_\_\_\_ pay the bill.

**B. Linking Sounds (consonant – vowel)** Listen carefully and complete these sentences. Mark the linking sounds.

> When a final consonant is followed by a vowel, the sounds are linked. The final consonant sounds like part of the next word.
> He work**s on** Saturday.

1.  Hoang _____ _____ college student.

2.  He _____ _____ part-time job.

3.  He needed money for his _____ _____ clothes.

4.  He _____ _____ _____ _____ Video World.

5.  He _____ _____ the evenings.

6.  He _____ _____ the weekends.

7.  Hoang is friendly _____ _____ the workers.

8.  I'd _____ _____ soda.

9.  He never saw his ten _____ _____ .

10. I _____ _____ haircut.

# CONVERSATIONS

**A. Match** Listen to these conversations. Each person wants to borrow something. Number each picture. Decide if the second speaker will lend the item. Circle *Yes* or *No*.

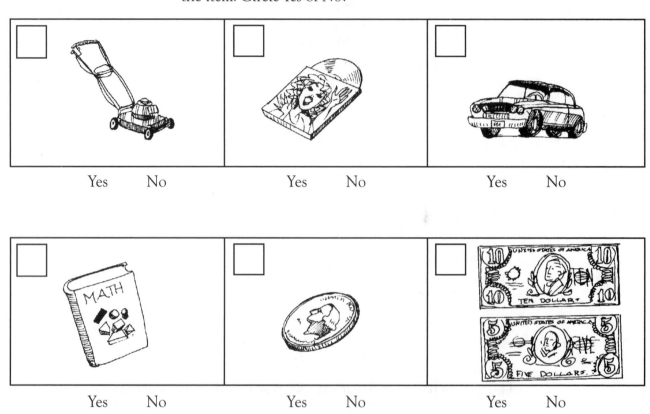

Yes    No          Yes    No          Yes    No

Yes    No          Yes    No          Yes    No

**B. Meaning** Listen to each sentence. Circle the letter of the sentence with the same meaning.

1.  a.  Do you need all of it?

    b.  Do you need any more?

2.  a.  I only need it for an hour.

    b.  I need it an hour from now.

3.  a.  My parents would be very

        angry.

    b.  My parents would not lend

        it to you.

4.  a.  You never give me your CDs.

    b.  You never returned my CD.

5.  a.  You used all the gas.

    b.  You broke it.

6.  a.  I'll return it on time.

    b.  I'll return it with gas in it.

**C. *Yes / No / Maybe*** One speaker is asking to borrow something. Decide if the second person is saying *yes*, *no*, or *maybe*. Circle *Yes*, *No*, or *Maybe*.

| | | | | | | |
|---|---|---|---|---|---|---|
| 1. Yes | No | Maybe | 5. Yes | No | Maybe |
| 2. Yes | No | Maybe | 6. Yes | No | Maybe |
| 3. Yes | No | Maybe | 7. Yes | No | Maybe |
| 4. Yes | No | Maybe | | | |

# INTERVIEWS

**In-Class Interview** Talk with a classmate about borrowing and lending.

*Did you ever borrow _____?*
*Who did you borrow it from?*
*How soon did you return it?*

| | Who? | How soon? |
|---|---|---|
| 1. a car | | |
| 2. a CD or tape | | |
| 3. a lawnmower | | |
| 4. ten dollars | | |
| 5. milk or eggs | | |
| 6. a book | | |
| 7. clothes | | |

**Out-of-Class Interview** Talk with a friend, neighbor, or coworker.

| | Who? | How soon? |
|---|---|---|
| 1. a car | | |
| 2. a CD or tape | | |
| 3. a lawnmower | | |
| 4. ten dollars | | |
| 5. milk or eggs | | |
| 6. a book | | |
| 7. clothes | | |

## 🗣 FACE TO FACE

**A.** STUDENT A: You need to borrow these five items. Ask Student B if you can borrow each one.

STUDENT B: Turn to page 141.

**B.** Now, change roles.

STUDENT A: Your neighbor is always borrowing things from you. You have decided not to lend this person anything else. Listen to each request from your neighbor. Then give an appropriate excuse from this list.

STUDENT B: Turn to page 141.

1. Sorry, I don't have any.
2. Sorry, I need it to get to work.
3. Sorry, it's broken.
4. Sorry, I'm broke.
5. Sorry, I need it to study for the test.

## INTERACTION

Sit with a partner. Practice several conversations in which you borrow or lend one of the items below. Explain why you want to borrow it. Your partner is happy to lend you most things. But there are a few items which your partner is hesitant to lend you or doesn't want to lend you. Act out one of your dialogues in front of the class.

# THE WORLD TRADE CENTER 12

## COMPREHENSION

**A. Before You Listen** Try to match these facts and figures about the World Trade Center. (Check your answers on page 129.)

1. _____ number of floors       a. 1,350
2. _____ height in feet       b. 50,000
3. _____ number of workers       c. 250
4. _____ number of daily visitors       d. 110
5. _____ number of elevators       e. 80,000

**B. Key Words** Discuss the new vocabulary, then complete the sentences below.

| | |
|---|---|
| **knocked out** | to disable a person or power source |
| **filled** | to take up space or room; to become full |
| **exploded** | to blow up with a loud noise and a strong force |
| **blow off – blew off** | to move with a strong current of air |
| **coughing** | to send out air from the lungs with a loud sound |
| **calm** | peaceful; not worried |

1. The bomb _____ in the basement.

2. The explosion _____ his hat.

3. Smoke quickly _____ the offices.

4. People did not scream and run; they stayed _____ .

5. The bomb _____ the electricity.

6. People were _____ from the heavy smoke.

**C. First Listening** Listen to this story about the bomb explosion at the World Trade Center. What were people doing at the time of the explosion? After you listen, tell the class any other information you remember about the event.

**D. Listen for the Facts** Listen to the story again. Complete this information about the event.

Date of blast: _____

Number of people working: _____

Time of blast: _____

Location of explosion: _____

Number of people who walked down the stairs: _____

**E. Comprehension Questions** Listen and circle the correct answer.

1. a. Yes, they did.
   b. No, they didn't.
2. a. at the beginning of the work day
   b. in the middle of the work day
   c. at the end of the work day
3. a. in the basement
   b. on the top floor
   c. in a cafeteria
4. a. the smoke from the fire
   b. the heat from the fire
   c. the flames from the fire
5. a. They waited for elevators.
   b. They waited for the fire department to rescue them.
   c. They walked down the stairs.
6. a. by running
   b. by singing
   c. by falling
7. a. Yes, they will.
   b. No, they won't.

# STRUCTURE

**A. Past Continuous Tense** Listen to these sentences. Write the past continuous verb you hear.

1. ___were working___       6. _____
2. _____        7. _____
3. _____        8. _____
4. _____        9. _____
5. _____        10. _____

# PRONUNCIATION

**A. Negative Contractions** Listen and complete these sentences with the negative contraction.

> In a negative contraction, we often do not hear the final **t** .
>
> were — weren't          is — isn't
>
> was — wasn't           did — didn't
>
> could — couldn't

1. The power _____ working.
2. There _____ any lights on the stairways.
3. She _____ sure what to do.
4. People _____ know what to do.
5. The elevators _____ work.
6. People _____ get out of the elevators.
7. There _____ any flames.
8. People _____ panic; they stayed calm.
9. He _____ going back into the building.
10. Some workers _____ return to work.

**B. Linking Sounds (consonant – vowel)** Listen carefully and complete these sentences. Mark the linking sounds.

> When a final consonant is followed by a vowel, the sounds are linked. The final consonant sounds like part of the next word.
> **Emergency workers were waiting with oxygen.**

1. Smoke began to fill the _____ _____ offices.
2. All power was _____ _____.
3. Many people _____ _____ their lunch break.
4. Some people were eating _____ _____ Windows on the World.
5. The bomb _____ _____ the basement area.
6. One woman _____ _____ the basement.
7. The bomb _____ _____ her shoes.
8. There were no _____ _____ the stairways.
9. I will never go _____ _____ there.
10. _____ _____ .

# CONVERSATIONS

🖿 **A. Match** Listen to these four people describe fires they saw. Number the pictures.

🖿 **B. True or False** Listen to each conversation again. Write *T* if the statement is true, *F* if the statement is false.

*Conversation 1*

1. _____ This speaker saw a car fire.

2. _____ This speaker never saw a real fire.

*Conversation 2*

3. _____ This speaker put a box of pizza in the oven.

4. _____ His mother knew the box was in the oven.

*Conversation 3*

5. _____ This speaker saw a large apartment building fire.

6. _____ Sixty to seventy people died in the fire.

*Conversation 4*

7. _____ You can't put metal in a microwave oven.

8. _____ This girl opened the microwave oven door immediately.

**C. And / But**   When telling a story in English, speakers frequently use *and* or *but* to connect ideas and to continue the conversation. Listen to these sentences. If you hear *and* or *but*, circle it. If you hear no connecting word, circle *c*.

| | | | | | |
|---|---|---|---|---|---|
| 1. a. and | b. but | c. | 6. a. and | b. but | c. |
| 2. a. and | b. but | c. | 7. a. and | b. but | c. |
| 3. a. and | b. but | c. | 8. a. and | b. but | c. |
| 4. a. and | b. but | c. | 9. a. and | b. but | c. |
| 5. a. and | b. but | c. | 10. a. and | b. but | c. |

# INTERVIEWS

**In-Class Interview**   Sit in a small group. Interview a student who has seen a fire.

| | |
|---|---|
| 1.  Did you ever see a fire? | |
| 2.  What was on fire? | |
| 3.  How large was the fire? | |
| 4.  How did the fire start? | |
| 5.  Was the fire department there? | |
| 6.  Was anything destroyed? | |
| 7.  Was anyone hurt? | |
| 8.  What did you do? | |

**Out-of-Class Interview**   Interview a friend, neighbor, or coworker who has seen a fire.

| | |
|---|---|
| 1.  Did you ever see a fire? | |
| 2.  What was on fire? | |
| 3.  How large was the fire? | |
| 4.  How did the fire start? | |
| 5.  Was the fire department there? | |
| 6.  Was anything destroyed? | |
| 7.  Was anyone hurt? | |
| 8.  What did you do? | |

## 👥 FACE TO FACE

STUDENT A: You and Student B both have pictures of a fire scene. There are seven differences in your pictures. Talk about your pictures. Try to find the differences. Do not look at your partner's picture.

STUDENT B: Turn to page 142.

# INTERACTION

Sit in a small group and discuss each of the situations below. As a group, cross out the things that each person should not do. Circle the things that each person should do and put them in order. Compare your answers with other groups.

Helen is cooking dinner at home. Only she and her three-year-old son are at home.

Hiro lives on the third floor of an apartment house. His friend sleeps in the next bedroom. Hiro just woke up. Smoke and flames are coming under his bedroom door.

_____ 1. Try to put out the fire.

_____ 2. Grab the baby and run out of the house.

_____ 3. Call the fire department from her house.

_____ 4. Call the fire department from her neighbor's house.

_____ 5. Go back in the house for the dog.

_____ 6. Go back in the house for the $1000 in cash in her bedroom.

_____ 1. Open the bedroom door.

_____ 2. Run into the next bedroom and wake up his friend.

_____ 3. Put a blanket under the door to stop or slow the smoke.

_____ 4. Bang on the wall and scream to wake up his friend.

_____ 5. Climb down the fire escape.

_____ 6. Try to walk down the stairs.

_____ 7. Call the fire department.

# THE TITANIC

## COMPREHENSION

**A. Before You Listen** Read the following sentences about icebergs. As a group, decide if each is true or false. Write *T* if the sentence is true, *F* if the sentence is false. (Check your answers on page 129.)

1. _____ An iceberg is a mountain of ice floating in the ocean.
2. _____ Icebergs break off from Greenland or Antarctica.
3. _____ Icebergs can be several miles long.
4. _____ Only the top part of an iceberg is above water. Most of it is under water.
5. _____ Icebergs are difficult to see, especially in the fog.
6. _____ Icebergs are no longer a danger to ships.

**B. Key Words** Discuss the new vocabulary, then complete the sentences below.

| | |
|---|---|
| **on board / aboard** | on a ship |
| **luxury** | very comfortable and expensive |
| **approaching** | coming near |
| **crewman** | a person who works on a ship |
| **ripped** | tore, made a hole in |
| **sink – sank** | to slowly fall to the bottom of a body of water |
| **lifeboats** | small open boats on a large ship, used in case of an accident or fire |
| **disaster** | a terrible event, often with the loss of many lives |

1. The ship _____ to the bottom of the ocean.
2. There were over two thousand people _____ the ship.
3. The first and only voyage of the Titanic ended as a _____ .
4. The iceberg _____ a large hole in the side of the ship.
5. There was no radar in the early 1900s. A _____ stood on the deck and watched for icebergs or other dangers.
6. The ship did not have enough _____ for all the passengers.
7. No one knew that the ship was _____ icebergs.
8. The _____ ship had dining rooms, a swimming pool, and libraries.

**C. First Listening** Listen to this story about the voyage of the Titanic. Who was Arthur Ryerson? What happened to him? After you listen, tell the class any other information you remember about the disaster.

**D. Listen for the Facts** Listen to the story again. Complete this information about the event.

1. Where did the Titanic leave from?

   _____

2. When did the Titanic pull out of port? _____

3. How many people were on board? _____

4. What was the date and time of the accident?

   _____

5. How large was the hole? _____

6. How many people lost their lives?_____

**E. Listen and Answer** Listen to these questions about what people were doing on the night of April 14. Write the number of the question in front of the correct answer.

_____ a. playing music

_____ b. sitting in the lifeboats

_____ c. sending out signals for help

_____ d. playing cards

_____ e. helping the women and children into the lifeboats

_____ f. still playing cards

_____ g. sleeping

**F. Comprehension Questions** Listen and circle the correct answer.

1. a. from New York to England
   b. from England to New York
   c. around the world

2. a. in the south Atlantic
   b. in the middle Atlantic
   c. in the north Atlantic

3. a. it was raining
   b. it was snowing
   c. it was clear

4. a. one of the crewmen
   b. one of the passengers
   c. Arthur Ryerson

5.  a.  the crew
    b.  the first people to reach them
    c.  the women and children

6.  a.  he continued to play cards
    b.  he helped the women and children into the life boats
    c.  he radioed for help

7.  a.  The water was cold.
    b.  The ship caught on fire.
    c.  There were not enough lifeboats.

# STRUCTURE

**A. Past Continuous Tense**  Listen to these sentences. Write the past continuous verb you hear.

1.  ___was carrying___
2.  _____
3.  _____
4.  _____
5.  _____
6.  _____
7.  _____
8.  _____
9.  _____
10. _____

# PRONUNCIATION

**A. Of**  Listen carefully and complete these sentences with *of* and the missing words.

> We often do not hear the **f** in the word *of.*
> Before a vowel or an **h, f** sounds like **v.**
>     the decks of the ship — the decks of the ship
>     of April — ov April
>     of his friends — ov his friends

1.  The Titanic pulled _____ _____ port on April 10, 1912.
2.  The first four _____ _____ the trip were clear and cold.
3.  Arthur Ryerson was playing cards with several _____ _____ friends.
4.  None of them _____ _____ the danger ahead.
5.  The evening _____ _____ 14 was relaxed.
6.  He was in a smoking room with three _____ _____ friends.
7.  _____ _____ the crewmen was standing watch.
8.  There was no room for _____ _____ the men.
9.  He returned to his _____ _____ cards.
10. It was _____ _____ the worst sea disasters in history.

**B. Word Stress** Listen carefully and mark the stressed words.

> The most important words in a sentence are stressed. They are longer and louder. These are the content words (nouns, verbs, adjectives, and adverbs).
>
> It was a **cóld níght.**

1. The Titanic was a luxury ship.

2. It was traveling from England to New York.

3. It was clear and cold.

4. The ship was approaching icebergs.

5. A crewman was standing watch.

6. He saw something in the water.

7. The ship hit an iceberg.

8. They radioed for help.

9. There was no panic.

10. The ship sank.

# SPEAKERS

**A. Match** Listen to each person describe one of the natural disasters below: a mud slide, a tornado, a hurricane, or an earthquake. Number each picture.

**B. Listen and Decide**  Listen and circle the letter of the idea that follows.

1. (a.) And when anyone saw one, they'd call.
   b. And we were supposed to go down into the basement.

2. a. And the town would blow this siren.
   b. Most of the time, we just saw them in the distance.

3. a. And they just exploded.
   b. One time, one hit the next town.

4. a. My dad drove us over there.
   b. There were no walls and no roofs.

5. a. So we worry about mud slides.
   b. Our bedroom is all windows.

6. a. And people around us began to get worried.
   b. Usually it's dry out here.

7. a. We have earthquake drills at school.
   b. That means we get under our desks.

8. a. And we put our heads between our legs.
   b. And they want us outside so that nothing can fall on us.

9. a. I remember watching the trees coming down.
   b. And we're not supposed to have hurricanes there.

10. a. I mean, huge trees coming down.
    b. School was closed all week.

**C. Past or Present**  Decide if the speaker is talking about a present situation or is describing an event that happened in the past. Circle *present* or *past*.

| | | | |
|---|---|---|---|
| 1. present    past | | 5. present    past | |
| 2. present    past | | 6. present    past | |
| 3. present    past | | 7. present    past | |
| 4. present    past | | 8. present    past | |

## INTERVIEWS

**In-Class Interview** Sit with another student or in a small group. Interview a student about an experience with a hurricane, earthquake, flood, tornado, or other natural disaster.

| | |
|---|---|
| 1. Did you ever see or experience a violent act of nature? Which one? | |
| 2. Where were you? | |
| 3. What were you doing at the time? | |
| 4. What happened? | |
| 5. Was anyone hurt? | |
| 6. Was there any damage to homes or buildings? | |
| 7. Were you able to prepare? | |
| 8. Were people evacuated? | |

**Out-of-Class Interview** Interview a friend, neighbor, or coworker about a similar experience.

| | |
|---|---|
| 1. Did you ever see or experience a violent act of nature? Which one? | |
| 2. Where were you? | |
| 3. What were you doing at the time? | |
| 4. What happened? | |
| 5. Was anyone hurt? | |
| 6. Was there any damage to homes or buildings? | |
| 7. Were you able to prepare? | |
| 8. Were people evacuated? | |

## FACE TO FACE

STUDENT A: You and Student B both have information about hurricanes, tornadoes, floods, and earthquakes. Ask and answer questions about each force of nature. Complete the information on page 109. Do not look at your partner's chart.

STUDENT B: Turn to page 143.

|  | Hurricanes | Tornadoes | Floods | Earthquakes |
|---|---|---|---|---|
| **Location** | along the southeastern coast of the U.S. |  | along rivers |  |
| **Time of year** |  | March through June |  | any time |
| **Length** | six days |  | several days |  |
| **Safest place** |  | in a basement |  | in an open area |
| **Warning** | several days |  | no warning to several hours |  |
| **Damage** |  | severe explosive wind damage |  | falling walls, objects, and roadways |

### Helpful Language

Where do most _____ occur?

What time of year do most _____ occur?

How long does a _____ last?

Where is the safest place to be during a _____ ?

Is there any warning of a _____ ?

What is the most serious damage from a _____ ?

## INTERACTION

Sit in a group of three students. There is a hurricane warning for your state. The hurricane will hit your town about 24 hours from now. You taped your windows and nailed large sheets of plywood over them. There is time to go to the store and buy supplies. These are the first three items on your list. Talk together and decide on five other items you need to buy.

1.  _____radio_____          5.  _____
2.  _____batteries_____      6.  _____
3.  _____candles_____        7.  _____
4.  _____          8.  _____

What would you do in case of a hurricane warning? Circle one of the choices below. Then explain your answer to your group.

a.  I would drive to a friend's house in another state.

b.  I would stay in my home.

c.  I would go to a school or other emergency shelter in my area.

d.  I would stay in my car.

e.  _____

## WHAT AND HOW TO RECYCLE

### *NEWSPAPERS*

√ Tie with twine in bundles no more than 12" high. *Do* **NOT** *use tape, wire or rubberbands to tie.*

√ **NO** *magazines, paper bags, telephone books or cardboard.*

### *GLASS BOTTLES AND JARS*

√ Rinse well.

√ Remove caps and lids.

√ Only bottles and jars will be collected.

√ **NO** *window glass, dishes, Pyrex, mirrors or crystal.*

### *CORRUGATED CARDBOARD*

√ Must be clean.

√ Must be flattened.

√ Must be tied in bundles.

√ **NO** *paper bags, magazines, telephone books, junk mail or newspapers.*

### *PLASTIC BOTTLES*

√ Rinse well.

√ Remove caps and lids.

√ All bottles should be flattened.

√ Only plastic bottles that contain pourable liquids, such as milk, soda, juice or detergent, will be accepted.

√ **NO** *squeeze bottles, packaging, plastic wrap or containers holding food or hazardous materials - such as motor oil or antifreeze.*

√ Acceptable materials will have a PET, PETE or HDPE mark or the number 1 or 2 in a triangle imprinted on the bottom of the bottle.

### *ALUMINUM & TIN CANS*

√ Must be well rinsed.

√ **NO** *paint cans or spray cans.*

# RECYCLING

## COMPREHENSION

**A. Before You Listen** Read each sentence about garbage disposal and recycling. Check those that are true about the city or town you live in.

_____ 1. We take our garbage to the local landfill.

_____ 2. A garbage truck picks up our garbage once or twice a week.

_____ 3. We burn our garbage.

_____ 4. Recycling is required in my town.

_____ 5. A special collection truck picks up recyclable materials in front of my home.

_____ 6. There is a recycling center in my town.

**B. Key Words** Discuss the new vocabulary, then complete the sentences below.

| | |
|---|---|
| **bury** | to dig a hole and put into the ground |
| **landfills** | areas where garbage is taken, with layers of garbage and earth |
| **trash** | garbage; the things that people throw away |
| **crush** | to break into small pieces |
| **separate** | to move apart; to put into different areas |
| **symbol** | a sign that represents an idea |
| **natural resources** | a country's wealth, in the form of oil, minerals, forests, etc. |

1. The tractors _____ the garbage down.

2. When you recycle, you need to _____ glass, plastic, and tin cans.

3. If people recycle, they can save _____ .

4. You can find the recycling _____ on the bottom of food containers.

5. In this country, most _____ is buried in landfills.

6. If you don't _____ the garbage, it smells terrible.

7. There are not enough _____ for all our garbage.

**C. First Listening** Listen to this story about recycling. What does the United States do with most of its garbage? Why is there a problem? After you listen, tell the class any other information you remember about the story.

**D. Second Listening** You will hear part of the story again. Put these pictures in order and explain what happened to the garbage from the town of Islip, Long Island.

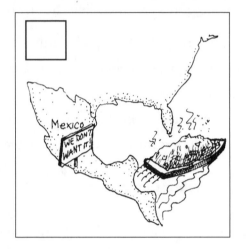

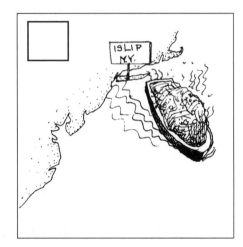

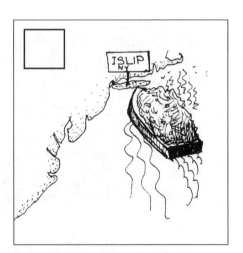

**E. Recycling** You will hear part of the story again. Write one use for each of these recycled products.

1. old aluminum cans _____

2. old glass bottles _____

3. old newspapers _____

4. old plastic _____

**F. Comprehension Questions** Listen and circle the correct answer.

1.  a. a lot of garbage
    b. a lot of money
    c. a lot of people

2.  a. It is burned.
    b. It is put in landfills.
    c. It is brought to other countries.

3.  a. because Islip doesn't have a landfill
    b. because it was on a boat
    c. because no one wanted it

4.  a. They should burn their garbage.
    b. They should pay other countries to take their garbage.
    c. There is not enough room for all their garbage.

5.  a. because recycling is the answer
    b. because the materials go to different factories
    c. because there is not enough room in landfills

6.  a. It saves trees and other natural resources.
    b. It saves energy.
    c. Both **a** and **b.**

7.  a. There is a recycling symbol on the bottom of the container.
    b. The product is made of paper or metal.
    c. The container says, "Please recycle."

# STRUCTURE

**A. Tense Contrast** Listen to these sentences. Write the verb you hear.

1.  _____empty_____        6.  _____
2.  _____         7.  _____
3.  _____         8.  _____
4.  _____         9.  _____
5.  _____         10. _____

# PRONUNCIATION

**A. Linking Sounds (Same Consonant)** Listen carefully and complete these sentences with the linked words. Mark the linking sounds.

> At times, the same sound or a similar sound is at the end of one word and at the beginning of the next word. The words are linked. We use the same sound for both words.
>
> The boat turned back to New York.

1. There was no _____ _____ in the landfill.

2. The _____ _____ , "No, thanks."

3. The captain _____ _____ pay Mexico.

4. The boat _____ _____ Florida.

5. New York City _____ _____ burn the garbage.

6. This _____ _____ woke people up.

7. _____ _____ require recycling.

8. We can all do a _____ _____ save the environment.

**B. Word Stress** Listen carefully to these questions and answers. Mark the stressed word(s) in the answer.

> We often stress the answer to a question, especially if the answer is in contrast to the question.
>
> Can I recycle window glass?
>
> No, you can only recycle **bóttles** and **járs.**

1. No, we have curbside pickup.

2. No, it comes every other week.

3. No, it comes on Monday.

4. No, it's free.

5. No, I recycle a lot of bottles.

6. No, we have a recycling center.

7. No, it's ten miles from here.

8. No, but we can recycle cardboard boxes.

9. No, we can put them in the same container.

10. No, we have to bring them to the conservation center.

# SPEAKERS

### 🔲 A. Match

These speakers are in an English conversation class. They are comparing garbage disposal and recycling in their countries and in the United States. Number the pictures.

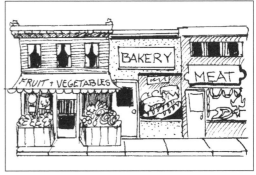

**B. True or False** Listen to each speaker again. Write *T* if the statement is true, *F* if the statement is false.

1. _____ This town has an open landfill.

2. _____ The garbage truck comes once every week.

3. _____ People keep their garbage in their houses.

4. _____ In this country, they recycle everything.

5. _____ People take bags with them when they go shopping.

6. _____ In this country, there are many supermarkets.

**C. Agree or Disagree** Listen to these statements about recycling. Compare them with recycling in your country. After you hear the statement, check one of the statements to show the situation in your country.

1. _____ We do the same in my country.

   _____ We don't do that in my country.

2. _____ It's that way in my country.

   _____ It's not that way in my country.

3. _____ We do the same in my country.

   _____ We don't do that in my country.

4. _____ It's like that in my country.

   _____ It's not like that in my country.

5. _____ We do, too.

   _____ We don't.

6. _____ It's like that in my country.

   _____ It's not like that in my country.

7. _____ It's similar in my country.

   _____ It's different in my country.

8. _____ It's that way in my country.

   _____ It's not that way in my country.

# INTERVIEWS

First, interview a student in this class. Then interview a friend, neighbor, or coworker. Ask these questions about recycling and saving our natural resources. Discuss your environmental habits. How can you or the person you interviewed do more to help save energy?

| Questions | In-Class Interview | Out-of-Class Interview |
|---|---|---|
| 1. Is there recycling collection in your town? | | |
| 2. Is there a recycling center in your town? | | |
| 3. Do you recycle newspapers? | | |
| 4. Do you recycle glass bottles? | | |
| 5. Do you recycle plastic bottles? | | |
| 6. Do you recycle cans? | | |
| 7. Do you ask for paper bags in the store? | | |
| 8. Do you check products you buy for the recycling symbol? | | |
| 9. In the summer, do you use the air conditioner 24 hours a day? | | |
| 10. In the winter, do you keep the thermostat at 68° or lower? | | |
| 11. Do you turn off the lights when you leave a room? | | |
| 12. Do you take showers that are five minutes or less? | | |
| 13. Do you use rechargeable batteries? | | |
| 14. Do you walk if you are only going a few blocks? | | |
| 15. Do you use Styrofoam cups? | | |

# 😃 FACE TO FACE

STUDENT A: Some materials are easy to recycle and make into other products. Other materials will take thousands of years or more to break down and decompose. Decide if products 1 to 8 are easy or difficult to recycle. Check *easy* or *difficult* next to each item. Ask Student B about each item. Then change roles. Student B will ask you about products 9 to 16.

STUDENT B: Turn to page 144.

| Product | Easy | Difficult |
|---|:---:|:---:|
| 1. aluminum cans | | |
| 2. newspapers | | |
| 3. batteries | | |
| 4. glass bottles | | |
| 5. aerosol cans | | |
| 6. tires | | |
| 7. oil paint | | |
| 8. paper bags | | |
| 9. metal (tin) cans | ✔ | |
| 10. cardboard boxes | ✔ | |
| 11. light bulbs | | ✔ |
| 12. magazines | | ✔ |
| 13. disposable diapers | | ✔ |
| 14. office paper | ✔ | |
| 15. plastic soda bottles | ✔ | |
| 16. Styrofoam cups | | ✔ |

**Helpful Language**

Is _____ easy to recycle?

Are _____s easy to recycle?

I think _____ is easy to recycle.

You're right. *or* No, it's difficult to recycle.

## INTERACTION

Below, six people are wasting energy or natural resources. Discuss how each person could save energy or resources. Write it under the picture. When you finish, your teacher will ask several groups to read their suggestions for each picture.

1. _____
   _____
   _____

2. _____
   _____
   _____

3. _____
   _____
   _____

4. _____
   _____
   _____

5. _____
   _____
   _____

6. _____
   _____
   _____

# DREAMS

## COMPREHENSION

**A. Before You Listen** Sit with a partner. Ask and answer questions about your dreams.

1. Did you dream last night? _____
2. Do you ever remember your dreams? _____
3. Do you ever dream about your childhood? _____
4. In your dreams, do you speak English? _____
5. Do you ever have nightmares (bad dreams)? _____

**B. Key Words** Discuss the new vocabulary, then complete the sentences below.

| | |
|---|---|
| **psychologist** | a doctor who studies the mind and behavior of people |
| **fear** | a thing that frightens or scares a person |
| **personality** | a person's character; manner of acting |
| **shy** | quiet; not comfortable in a group |
| **stand for** | to represent; be an example of something else |
| **failure** | not successful |

1. I have a _____ of snakes.

2. They are seeing a _____ to talk about their family problems.

3. She fights for what she wants; she has an aggressive _____ .

4. In a dream, a queen might _____ a person's mother.

5. He's worried that the new business might be a _____ .

6. My sister is _____ when she meets new people.

**C. First Listening** Listen to this story about dreams. What do dreams mean? After you listen, tell the class any other information you remember about the story.

▭ **D. Second Listening**  Listen to these statements. Circle *T* if the statement is true, *F* if the statement is false.

1. T  F          5. T  F
2. T  F          6. T  F
3. T  F          7. T  F
4. T  F          8. T  F

▭ **E. Matching**  Listen to the story again. Match each symbol with an idea that it might represent.

____ 1.

a.  fear of failure

____ 2.

b.  a father

____ 3.

c.  death

____ 4.

d.  hope that you will
    be successful

____ 5.

e.  children

# STRUCTURE

**A. *Might*** Listen to these sentences. Write the complete verb you hear.

1. ___ might see ___    6. _____
2. _____          7. _____
3. _____          8. _____
4. _____          9. _____
5. _____         10. _____

# PRONUNCIATION

**A. Word Stress** Listen carefully and mark the stressed word in each pair.

> Stress can put special emphasis on any word in a sentence. Stress can change the meaning of the sentence.
> I **néver** dream.
> **Í** never dream.

1. a. He snores all night.
   b. He snores all night.

2. a. You should go to bed earlier.
   b. You should go to bed earlier.

3. a. I want to hear about your dream.
   b. I want to hear about your dream.

4. a. What's the meaning of that dream?
   b. What's the meaning of that dream?

5. a. Dreams can be frightening.
   b. Dreams can be frightening.

6. a. I can't tell her my dream.
   b. I can't tell her my dream.

7. a. I never have nightmares.
   b. I never have nightmares.

**B. _Do / Did_** Listen to these questions about sleep and dreams. Circle the first two words of each question, _Do you_ or _Did you._

_Did you_ often sounds like _Didja._

Did you dream last night? — Didja dream last night?

_Do you_ often sounds like _Dya._

Do you dream a lot? — Dya dream a lot?

| | | | | | | |
|---|---|---|---|---|---|---|
| 1. | Do you | Did you | | 6. | Do you | Did you |
| 2. | Do you | Did you | | 7. | Do you | Did you |
| 3. | Do you | Did you | | 8. | Do you | Did you |
| 4. | Do you | Did you | | 9. | Do you | Did you |
| 5. | Do you | Did you | | 10. | Do you | Did you |

## DREAMS

**A. Match** Listen to these six people describe their dreams. Number the pictures.

**B. Meaning** Listen to each dream again. Circle the letter of the correct sentence.

1. In this dream, the speaker
   a. is washing windows.
   b. is watching his father.
   c. is screaming.

2. This person
   a. is pregnant.
   b. wants to be pregnant.
   c. doesn't want to be pregnant.

3. This person
   a. had one long dream.
   b. dreamed the exact same dream three times.
   c. dreamed about the same situation three times.

4. In this dream, the person
   a. was running for exercise.
   b. was running away from an animal.
   c. was running away from her husband.

5. In this dream, the person
   a. finds a little money.
   b. finds a lot of money.
   c. steals some money.

6. In this dream, the children
   a. help the young woman.
   b. get in a boat.
   c. watch the woman go past.

**C. Dream Interpretations** Sit in a small group. The teacher will play the tape again. Your group has three minutes to talk and to write one possible meaning, or interpretation, for each dream. Compare your ideas, then continue with the next dream. One possible meaning is given for the first dream.

1. _____ **He's worried about his father's health.** _____

2. _____

3. _____

4. _____

5. _____

6. _____

# INTERVIEWS

**In-Class Interview** Interview a classmate about sleeping habits.

| | |
|---|---|
| 1. What time do you go to bed? | |
| 2. What time do you get up? | |
| 3. Are you tired when you wake up? | |
| 4. Do you need an alarm clock to wake you up? | |
| 5. Is it easy for you to fall asleep? | |
| 6. Do you read before you go to sleep? | |
| 7. Do you take a hot bath before you go to sleep? | |
| 8. Do you wake up during the night? | |
| 9. Do you snore? | |
| 10. Are you a heavy or a light sleeper? | |

**Out-of-Class Interview** Interview a friend, neighbor, or coworker about sleeping habits.

| | |
|---|---|
| 1. What time do you go to bed? | |
| 2. What time do you get up? | |
| 3. Are you tired when you wake up? | |
| 4. Do you need an alarm clock to wake you up? | |
| 5. Is it easy for you to fall asleep? | |
| 6. Do you read before you go to sleep? | |
| 7. Do you take a hot bath before you go to sleep? | |
| 8. Do you wake up during the night? | |
| 9. Do you snore? | |
| 10. Are you a heavy or a light sleeper? | |

# INTERACTION I

Sit in a small group of three or four students. Decide on a possible meaning for each of the dream symbols below. Use your imagination. Under each picture, write two things it might stand for. Share your ideas with the other groups.

1. _____

2. _____

3. _____

4. _____

### *Helpful Language*

It might stand for a _____ .

It might represent a _____ .

It might be a symbol of/for _____ .

It might mean that _____ .

## INTERACTION II

Sit with a partner. In the box below, draw a picture of one of your dreams. Then, tell your partner about the dream. Try to remember as many details as possible. Your partner will try to interpret your dream.

*This Answer Key provides answers for selected exercises.*

## UNIT 2

### Before You Listen *(page 11)*

1. False   About one out of every five Americans smokes.
2. True
3. False   About 150,000 Americans a year die of lung cancer.
4. True
5. True
6. True

## UNIT 3

### Before You Listen *(page 19)*

Senior citizens are most likely to go to a store, the home of a relative or friend, and to a restaurant.

## UNIT 10

### Before You Listen *(page 77)*

| | |
|---|---|
| Leif Ericson lands in North America. | 1000 |
| Marco Polo visits China. | 1275 |
| Ferdinand Magellan sails around the world. | 1521 |
| Charles Lindbergh flies from New York to Paris. | 1927 |
| Yuri Gagarin travels in space. | 1961 |
| Neil Armstrong walks on the moon. | 1969 |

## UNIT 12

### Before You Listen *(page 95)*

1. d.  110
2. a.  1,350
3. b.  50,000
4. e.  80,000
5. c.  250

## UNIT 13

### Before You Listen *(page 103)*

1. True
2. True
3. True
4. True
5. True
6. False

## UNIT 1

### 👥 FACE TO FACE

STUDENT A:  Turn to page 8.

STUDENT B:  The incomplete chart below gives information about four people and their jobs. Student A has the missing information. Ask and answer questions about these four people. Complete the information.

---

1.

PLACE: _____
JOB: ___waiter_____
HOURS: _____
SALARY: ___$3.00 an hour + tips_____
BENEFITS: _____
OPINION: _____

2.

PLACE: ___Tektron_____
JOB: _____
HOURS: _____
SALARY: __$47,000 a year_____
BENEFITS: _____
OPINION: _She likes the job._____

3.

PLACE: _____
JOB: ____x-ray technician_____
HOURS: __7 A.M. to 3 P.M._____
SALARY: _____
BENEFITS: _medical, 2 weeks vacation_
OPINION: _____

4.

PLACE: ___Carney Library_____
JOB: _____
HOURS: __12 P.M. to 9 P.M._____
SALARY: _____
BENEFITS: _____
OPINION: _He likes the job, but he doesn't
           like his boss._____

---

### *Helpful Language*

Where does he work?
What does he do?
What hours does he work?

What's his salary?
What benefits does he have?
Does he like his job?

## UNIT 2

### 👥 FACE TO FACE

STUDENT A: Turn to page 16.

STUDENT B: Read these ten sentences about smoking to Student A. Student A will check if she agrees or disagrees with each statement, and tell you her opinion. Then change roles. Turn to page 16. Listen and check your opinion.

When you both finish, discuss the statements that you don't have the same opinion about. Give your reasons.

1. It's easy to stop smoking.
2. People who smoke should pay higher health insurance.
3. All restaurants should have a non-smoking section.
4. There should be a dollar tax on each pack of cigarettes.
5. Children get sick from their parents' cigarette smoke.
6. Most smokers want to quit.
7. Cigarette smoke makes a person's clothes smell.
8. It's too easy for children to buy cigarettes.
9. There should be no smoking in bars.
10. Smokers have less energy than non-smokers.

### *Helpful Language*

| | |
|---|---|
| I agree completely. | I don't agree with that. |
| I feel the same. | I don't think that's right. |
| Definitely. | I don't think so. |
| Absolutely. | That's wrong. |
| That's just what I think. | |

# UNIT 3

## 👥 FACE TO FACE

STUDENT A: Turn to page 25.

STUDENT B: Give Student A a few minutes to read numbers 1 to 8 and circle the correct answer. Then, Student A will ask you questions about these facts. Read the answer. Change roles. Read numbers 9 to 16 and circle the answer you think is correct. Check your answers with Student A. Begin each question with the words in parentheses.

1. *Women* live longer.
2. The life expectancy for men is *72*.
3. The life expectancy for women is *80*.
4. *Japan* has the highest life expectancy.
5. *Thirteen percent* of the population of the US is over 65.
6. *California* has the highest number of senior citizens.
7. *Florida* has the highest percentage of senior citizens.
8. Most senior citizens live *at home*.

9. The major source of income for people over 65 is _____ . (What?)
   a. Social Security    b. savings    c. a pension

10. Most senior citizens describe their health as _____ . (How?)
    a. poor    b. good    c. excellent

11. The most common medical condition for seniors is _____ . (What?)
    a. arthritis    b. high blood pressure    c. hearing problems

12. Most senior citizens see their children _____ . (How often?)
    a. every day    b. once a week    c. once a month

13. _____ of the elderly live in nursing homes. (What percentage?)
    a. about four percent    b. ten percent    c. seventeen percent

14. The favorite leisure time activity for seniors is _____ . (What?)
    a. walking    b. reading    c. watching TV

15. The most common cause of death for senior citizens is _____ . (What?)
    a. heart disease    b. cancer    c. accidents

16. Senior citizens say their biggest problem is _____ . (What?)
    a. health    b. crime    c. the high cost of living

## UNIT 4

## 👥 FACE TO FACE

STUDENT A: Turn to page 32.

STUDENT B: The chart below gives information about Apartment 2. Student A has the information about Apartment 1. Ask and answer questions about the apartments. Complete the missing information.

|  | **Apartment 1** | **Apartment 2** |
|---|---|---|
| Address |  | 515 Mountain Avenue |
| Bedrooms |  | 2 |
| Baths |  | 1 |
| Rent |  | $575 a month |
| Utilities |  | not included |

### *Helpful Language*

Where is the apartment?

How many bedrooms are there?

How many bathrooms are there?

What's the rent?

Are the utilities included?

Please repeat that.

Please repeat the address.

Excuse me. (repeat the question)

## UNIT 5

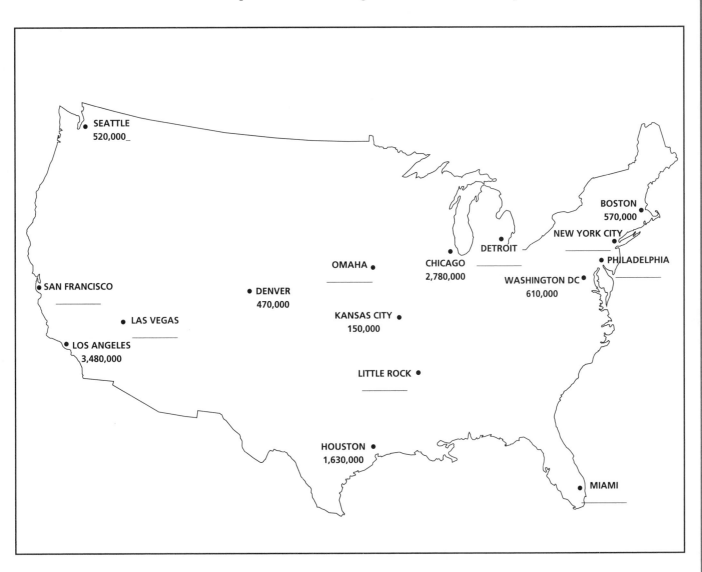 **FACE TO FACE**

STUDENT A:  Turn to page 40.

STUDENT B:  The map below gives the population of several major cities. Student A will ask about the population of these cities. Then change roles. Ask Student A about the population of the other cities on your map. Write the missing information on the map.

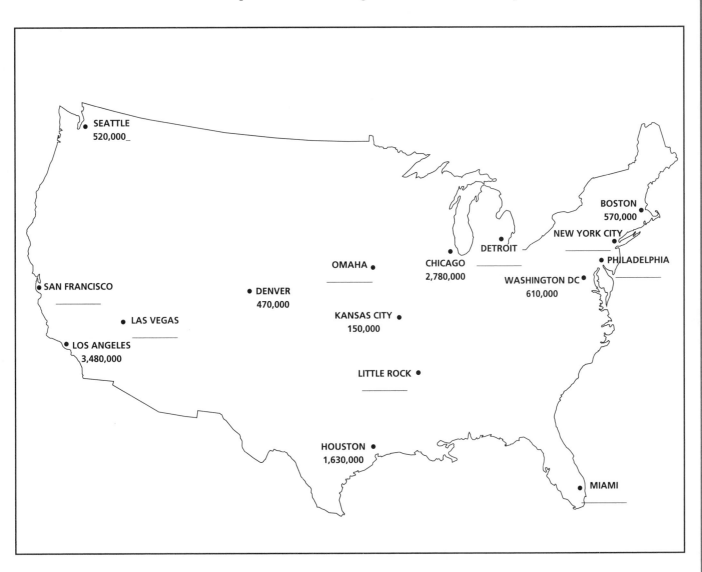

***Helpful Language***

What's the population of ___(city)___ ?

Please repeat that number.

Excuse me?

Is that ___(number)___ ?

## UNIT 6

## 👥 FACE TO FACE

STUDENT A: Turn to page 48.

STUDENT B: The incomplete chart below gives the average salary and outlook for 15 jobs. You have the information about half the jobs. Student A has the information about the other half. Ask and answer questions about the average salary and outlook for each job. Fill in the missing information.

| | Job | Average Salary | Outlook |
|---|---|---|---|
| 1. | accountant | $24,000–$35,000 | very good |
| 2. | physical therapist | _____ | _____ |
| 3. | telephone installer | $24,000 | poor |
| 4. | mechanical engineer | _____ | _____ |
| 5. | pharmacist | $31,000–$44,000 | very good |
| 6. | social worker | _____ | _____ |
| 7. | family doctor | $98,000 | excellent |
| 8. | jeweler | _____ | _____ |
| 9. | real estate agent | $24,000–$30,000 | good |
| 10. | funeral director | _____ | _____ |
| 11. | plumber | $23,000–$29,000 | good |
| 12. | electrical technician | _____ | _____ |
| 13. | carpenter | $23,000 | good |
| 14. | dentist | _____ | _____ |
| 15. | professional athlete | $25,000–$5,000,000 | poor |

### Helpful Language

What's the average salary for a/an __(job)__ ?

A/An __(job)__ earns / makes about $ _____ a year.

A/An __(job)__ earns / makes between $ _____ and
$ _____ a year.

What's the job outlook for a/an __(job)__

# UNIT 7

## FACE TO FACE

STUDENT A: Turn to page 56.

STUDENT B: You and Student A both have pictures of an accident scene. There are seven differences in your pictures. Talk about your pictures. Try to find the differences. Do not look at your partner's picture.

## UNIT 8

### FACE TO FACE

STUDENT A: Turn to page 66.

STUDENT B: Yesterday a thief broke into Kim's apartment. You have a picture of Kim's apartment after it was robbed. Student A has a picture of Kim's apartment before it was robbed. Talk together about the contents of the apartment and decide what items were taken. Make a list of the eight items that the thief stole. Do not look at Student A's picture.

1. _____   5. _____

2. _____   6. _____

3. _____   7. _____

4. _____   8. _____

### Helpful Language

Yes, he took it.          No, he didn't take it.

Yes, it's still there.     No, it isn't there anymore.

Was there anything (on the night table)?

## UNIT 9

### 👥 FACE TO FACE

STUDENT A: Turn to page 74.

STUDENT B: This picture shows twelve people who won the lottery. You and Student A have information about how six different people spent their winnings. Ask and answer questions about these winners. Draw a line from each person to the action.

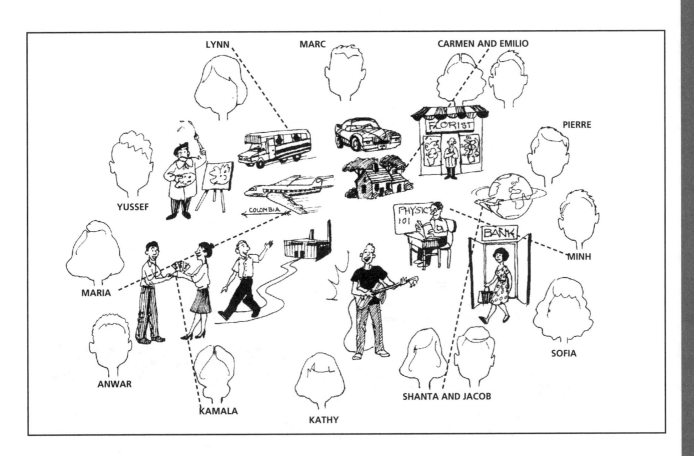

***Helpful language***

What did _____ do with the money?

## UNIT 10

### 👥 FACE TO FACE

STUDENT A: Turn to page 84.

STUDENT B: You have a picture of a computer with six parts labeled:

7. disk drive
8. disk
9. printer
10. printer cable
11. CD ROM player
12. CD disk

Student A has the same computer with six different parts labeled. Talk about the computer, naming and describing the parts. Try to label all the parts of the computer.

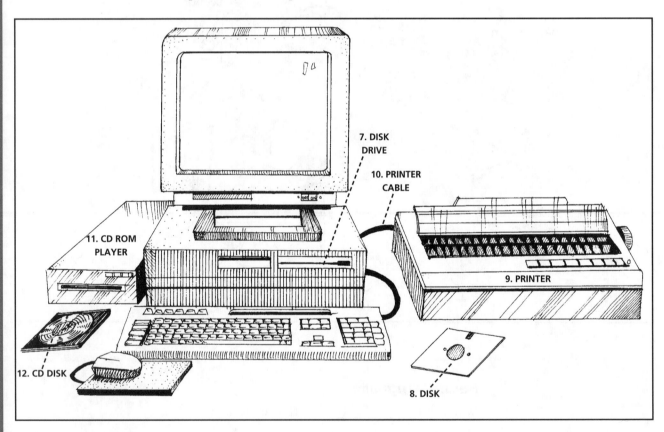

### *Helpful Language*

Number 1 is the monitor.

Where's the monitor?

It's on (under, next to, in front of) the computer.

What's a monitor?

It's like a TV screen. you see words or pictures on it.

How do you spell monitor?

## UNIT 11

### 👥 FACE TO FACE

**A.** STUDENT A: Turn to page 92.

STUDENT B: Your neighbor is always borrowing things from you. You have decided not to lend this person anything else. Listen to each request from your neighbor. Then give an appropriate excuse from this list.

1. Sorry, someone stole it.

2. Sorry, we're having a barbecue tonight.

3. Sorry, I need to cut the grass, too.

4. Sorry, I'm broke.

5. Sorry, I don't have any.

**B.** Now, change roles.

STUDENT A: Turn to page 92.

STUDENT B: You need to borrow these five items. Ask Student A if you can borrow each one.

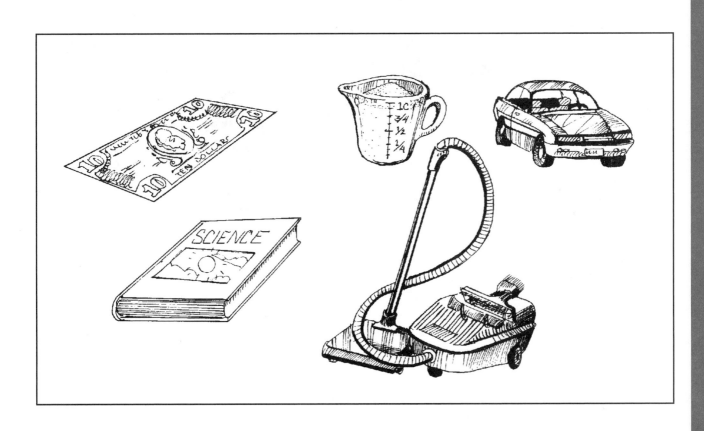

## UNIT 12

### FACE TO FACE

STUDENT A: Turn to page 100.

STUDENT B: You and Student A both have pictures of a fire scene. There are seven differences in your pictures. Talk about your pictures. Try to find the differences. Do not look at your partner's picture.

# UNIT 13

## 👥 FACE TO FACE

STUDENT A: Turn to pages 108–109.

STUDENT B: You and Student A both have information about hurricanes, tornadoes, floods, and earthquakes. Ask and answer questions about each force of nature. Complete the information below. Do not look at your partner's chart.

|  | Hurricanes | Tornadoes | Floods | Earthquakes |
|---|---|---|---|---|
| **Location** |  | in the midwest |  | in the western part of the U.S. |
| **Time of year** | late summer and early fall |  | after a heavy rain |  |
| **Length** |  | 30 to 60 minutes |  | a few seconds to a few minutes |
| **Safest place** | inside a strong building |  | on high ground |  |
| **Warning** |  | no warning or a short warning |  | no warning |
| **Damage** | heavy wind damage to homes and trees |  | rising water, drowning |  |

### *Helpful Language*

Where do most _____ occur?

What time of year do most _____ occur?

How long does a _____ last?

Where is the safest place to be during a _____ ?

Is there any warning of a _____ ?

What is the most serious damage from a _____ ?

## UNIT 14

### 👥 FACE TO FACE

STUDENT A: Turn to page 118.

STUDENT B: Some materials are easy to recycle and make into other products. Other materials will take thousands of years or more to break down and decompose. Student A will ask you about products 1 to 8. Then decide if products 9 to 16 are easy or difficult to recycle. Check *easy* or *difficult* next to each item. Ask Student A about each item.

Change roles.

| Product | Easy | Difficult |
|---|---|---|
| 1. aluminum cans | ✔ | |
| 2. newspapers | ✔ | |
| 3. batteries | | ✔ |
| 4. glass bottles | ✔ | |
| 5. aerosol cans | | ✔ |
| 6. tires | | ✔ |
| 7. oil paint | | ✔ |
| 8. paper bags | ✔ | |
| 9. metal (tin) cans | | |
| 10. cardboard boxes | | |
| 11. light bulbs | | |
| 12. magazines | | |
| 13. disposable diapers | | |
| 14. office paper | | |
| 15. plastic soda bottles | | |
| 16. Styrofoam cups | | |

### *Helpful Language*

Is _____ easy to recycle?

Are _____s easy to recycle?

I think _____ is easy to recycle.

You're right.  *or*  No, it's difficult to recycle.

**FACE TO FACE: Student B**

# UNIT 1:  Do You Like Your Job?

## COMPREHENSION

**Page 3**

**Story**

I'm a toll collector on the Turnpike. I've been working there for seven years and I really like the job. I stand or sit on a stool and take the tolls from drivers. There's always a line so I have to work fast. The work is interesting and I'm always busy. Drivers need change or they want to buy tokens. Sometimes they ask for directions or want to know the weather conditions on the road ahead. I can recognize every make and model of car and I see some beautiful ones, Rolls Royces, Lambourghinis, Ferraris.

My hours are great, from 11:00 P.M. to 7 A.M., so I can work after I put the children in bed. If I want, there's lots of overtime, especially on the weekends. The pay is good and I have medical benefits for myself and my family. I feel lucky to have this job.

---

I'm a toll collector on the Turnpike. I've been working there for a year and I really hate the job. The work is boring. I just stand in a small booth and collect fifty cents or a token. It's the same thing over and over for eight or nine hours. In the winter, I'm always cold, especially my fingers. In the summer I'm always hot because there's no air conditioning. Also, I hate the smell of car fumes. The smell of gas gives me a headache.

My hours are terrible, from 11:00 P.M. to 7 A.M. I can't go out with my friends because I have to be home by 10:00 to get ready for work. My boss is never satisfied. He complains that I work too slowly. And there's no opportunity for a promotion. I don't want to collect tolls for the next thirty years. It's time to look for a new job.

**Page 4**

**E. *Like / Doesn't like*** You will hear ten sentences. Decide if the speaker is describing something he likes or doesn't like about his job.

1. My hours are terrible.
2. The work is interesting and I'm always busy.
3. My hours are great.
4. The work is boring.
5. My boss always complains about my work.
6. The pay is good.
7. There's no opportunity for promotion.
8. It's the same thing over and over.
9. If I want, I can work lots of overtime.
10. In the winter, I'm always cold. In the summer, I'm always hot.

## STRUCTURE

**Page 4**

**A. Present Tense** Listen to these sentences. Write the present tense verb you hear.

1. I really hate the job.
2. I collect fifty cents.
3. The smell of gas gives me a headache.
4. My boss complains about my work.
5. I don't like my job.
6. I take tolls from drivers.
7. Many drivers buy tokens.
8. Drivers ask for directions.
9. I recognize every make and model of car.
10. I have medical benefits.

**Page 4**

**B. *Always / Never*** Look at the explanation about the placement of *always* and *never*. Read the sentences on page 5. Stop the tape and put a star (*) at the correct place for *always* or *never*. Then, listen to the sentences and check your answers.

1. I never work overtime.
2. I am never late for work.
3. The boss always complains about my work.
4. The boss always gives me good evaluations.
5. I am never bored at work.
6. I am always tired after eight hours.
7. The boss is never satisfied with my work.
8. I always enjoy talking with people.
9. I am never going to quit this job.
10. The boss never gives me overtime.

## PRONUNCIATION

**Page 5**

**A. *And / Or*** Listen carefully and complete the sentences with *and* or *or*.

> *And* often sounds like *ǝnd*. *Or* often sounds like *ǝr*.
> My hands *ǝnd* feet are cold.
> I can't see my family *ǝr* friends.

1. I sit or stand.
2. I usually work on Saturday and Sunday.
3. I can recognize every make and model.
4. I sometimes see a Lambourghini or a Rolls Royce.
5. I have medical benefits for myself and my family.
6. I collect money or a token.
7. It's the same thing over and over.
8. I work eight or nine hours a night.
9. In the winter, the work is cold and boring.
10. I'm going to quit and find a new job.

**Page 5**

**B. *Don't*** In spoken English, it is sometimes difficult to hear *don't*. Listen carefully and circle the sentence you hear.

1. I don't like my job.
2. I work a lot of overtime.
3. I don't think the work is interesting.
4. I have medical benefits.
5. I don't work during the day.
6. I don't like to work in the cold weather.
7. I don't want to stay here.
8. I need to look for another job.

## CONVERSATIONS

**Page 6**

### Conversation 1

A: Where do you work?
B: At Union County College.
A: What do you do?
B: I work in the Learning Center. I'm a math tutor. You know, I help students with their math and algebra.
A: How do you like your job?
B: I like it a lot. I like to talk to people and help them. And my hours are flexible. I put in twenty hours a week, sometimes in the morning, sometimes in the afternoon, whenever they need me.
B: Is there anything you don't like?
A: Well, I'm just a student, so I only get minimum wage. But that's fine for now. I'm happy I have a job.

### Conversation 2

A: I got a job at United Electrical.
B: Great! What do you do there?
A: I work on new homes. I do the wiring, you know, lights, doorbells, outlets.
B: How's your boss?
A: He's good. He's clear about exactly what to do.
B: Sounds like you found a good job.
A: Yeah, so far everything's fine. My only problem is medical benefits. I don't get any medical benefits for six months, and then they're just for me. I have to pay extra for my wife and little boy.

### Conversation 3

A: So you're the first woman they hired?
B: Yes, there are ten men, ten car salesmen, and me.
A: And how are you doing?
B: This week, I sold three cars. I was the top salesperson.
A: How do you do it? Do you do anything special?
B: No, not really. It helps that I'm a woman. There are a lot of women looking at cars and buying cars by themselves. A lot of them feel more comfortable talking to a woman. You know me, I like to talk.
A: How are the other salesmen?

B: Most of them are friendly. But there are two or three who don't talk to me. And at lunch, when two or three go out together, they never ask me.
A: It's going to take time.
B: Yeah. I think it's going to take a long time.

### Conversation 4

A: Carl, someone told me that you're a photographer.
B: Yeah, I have my own business.
A: What kind of photography?
B: Well, the biggest part of the business is weddings, so I work most Saturdays and Sundays. I also do personal photos, you know, like baby pictures, family photos, passport photos.
A: So, you're your own boss.
B: Hmm-hmm. Maybe my hours are crazy, but I can decide which jobs to take.

**Page 7**

**C. *How*** Listen to these *How* questions. Circle the appropriate answer.

1. How's your job?
2. How's your boss?
3. How are your hours?
4. How are your benefits?
5. How are the other workers?
6. How's business?

# UNIT 2: My Mom Smokes

## COMPREHENSION

**Page 11**

### Story

My mom smokes a lot. She always has a cigarette in her hand. As soon as she wakes up, she reaches for her cigarettes on the night table. She smokes before breakfast, after breakfast and when she drives us to school. She works in an office but she can't smoke there. So she smokes in the employees' lounge at break and after lunch. And she smokes in the evening at home, especially when she watches TV.

Mom is the only one in our family that smokes. We all hate it. The house smells and everybody's clothes smell and her breath smells. She doesn't have a lot of energy. As soon as she tries to exercise, she becomes short of breath. And my little sister, Katie, gets bad coughs all the time.

Mom's tried to quit. She went to a Stop Smoking program and she stopped for a while. And once she was hypnotized, but that didn't work. She says she wants to stop, but she can't.

Tomorrow I'm going to be twelve. My mom asked me, "What do you want for your birthday?" You know what I answered? "I only want one thing, for you to stop smoking."

Page 12

### E. Comprehension Questions   Listen and circle the correct answer.

1. How many cigarettes does this woman smoke a day?
2. Is smoking permitted at this woman's work?
3. How does her daughter feel?
4. Does anyone else in the family smoke?
5. What is the most serious effect of her smoking?
6. How has smoking affected this woman's health?
7. Does this woman want to stop smoking?

## STRUCTURE

Page 12

### A. Tense Contrast   Listen to these sentences. Decide the tense of the verb. Circle *present* or *past*.

1. My mom always has a cigarette in her hand.
2. She smokes before breakfast.
3. She works in an office.
4. She smokes in the employees' lounge.
5. She tried to quit.
6. She went to a Stop Smoking program.
7. She stopped for a while.
8. The house smells from the smoke.
9. She wants to stop.
10. She stopped for a while, but she started again.

Page 13

### B. Negatives   Listen to these sentences. Write the negative verb.

1. Her family doesn't like her to smoke.
2. She doesn't smoke at her desk.
3. She doesn't have a lot of energy.
4. She doesn't know how to stop.
5. Her children don't smoke.
6. Her husband doesn't smoke.
7. The children don't want her to smoke.
8. She doesn't exercise.
9. The children don't like the smell of smoke.
10. Don't begin to smoke.

## PRONUNCIATION

Page 13

### A. Same or Different   You will hear two verbs. Decide if they are the same or different. Circle *same* or *different*.

1. smoke – smokes
2. drive – drive
3. hate – hates
4. smells – smells
5. reach – reaches
6. have – has
7. works – works
8. watches – watches
9. want – wants
10. wake – wakes

Page 13

### B. Linking with *-s*   Listen carefully and complete these sentences with the missing words. Mark the linking sounds.

> When a final *-s* is followed by a vowel, the sounds are linked. The *-s* sounds like part of the next word.
>
> My mom **has a** problem.

1. My mom smokes a lot.
2. She always has a cigarette in her hand.
3. She smokes all day.
4. She starts as soon as she wakes up.
5. She lights up a cigarette after breakfast.
6. She works in an office.
7. She smokes in the employees' lounge.
8. She buys a pack of cigarettes a day.
9. My little sister coughs all the time.
10. My mom smokes in bed.

## CONVERSATIONS

Page 14

### Conversation 1

A: Excuse me. There's no smoking in the waiting room.
B: I don't see a sign.
A: It's here, on the window.
B: Oh.

### Conversation 2

A: Excuse me, ma'am. There's no smoking allowed on domestic flights.
B: But I could always smoke in the last five rows.
A: Not anymore. That changed a few years ago.

### Conversation 3

A: Excuse me. Could you put out your cigarette?
B: I can smoke here.
A: Well, I'm eating my lunch and I can't taste anything when someone's smoking.
B: Sorry, but this is the only place in this building where smoking is allowed.

### Conversation 4

A: You promised me you wouldn't smoke on the way there.
B: Just one.
A: I hate the smell.
B: We can roll down the windows.
A: Please don't.

### Conversation 5

A: Charlie, smoke in your own office.
B: Come on, Mary. What's a little smoke?
A: Look, I don't smoke, and I don't want anyone else to smoke in here.

**Conversation 6**

A: Excuse me, you can't smoke in here.

B: I'm just going to be in here for a minute. I need to take out this book.

A: This is a public building. Put out your cigarette or leave.

B: OK. OK.

**Page 14**

**B. Same or Different**  Read each sentence. Then, listen and decide if the meaning is the same or different. Circle S or *D*.

1. Smoke in your own office.
2. Just one.
3. This is the only place in the building where smoking is allowed.
4. We can roll down the windows.
5. Not anymore.
6. I could always smoke here before.

**Page 15**

**C. Smoking Situations**  You will hear some common questions that smokers and non-smokers ask. How would *you* answer?

1. Do you smoke?
2. Is it OK if I smoke here?
3. Mind if I smoke?
4. Would you like a cigarette?
5. Could you put out your cigarette?
6. Do you have a cigarette?
7. Do you have a light?
8. Would you like smoking or non-smoking?

# UNIT 3: Adult Day Care

## COMPREHENSION

**Page 19**

**Story**

David Brown and Ann Ramos are two patients participating in the Adult Day-Care program at Mercy Hospital.

David Brown is 72 years old. He's friendly and likes to talk. He lives with his wife in a small apartment in the city. But David is becoming forgetful. His wife says, "He'll heat up some soup, then forget to turn off the stove." She's 61 and still works. She worries about leaving her husband alone by himself.

Ann Ramos is 80 and lives with her daughter, who is 60. Her daughter says that she needs a break. "Mom follows me everywhere. She follows me from room to room when I clean. She sits down next to me when I read the newspaper. She even follows me out of the house when I take out the garbage. I need a break and she does, too."

And so, several times a week, David and Ann's families take them to the Adult Day-Care Center. Many hospitals now offer this program. Patients come to the center for a full or half day, from one to five days a week. All the patients live with their families and most are elderly. Some are becoming forgetful, others are recovering from an operation, a stroke, or an accident. The Center offers many activities. Patients learn crafts, such as sewing and painting. Many patients like to cook and they bake fresh bread. Several men and women enjoy playing checkers, bingo, cards, or other games. All the patients enjoy talking, singing, and being with one another.

Some patients also need physical therapy. One woman had a stroke and can't move her right arm. She's doing simple exercises and the movement is slowly returning.

The Center offers both the patients and their families a valuable service. Patients are able to get out of their homes. Husbands, wives, or grown children can work or have a break. Most important, families are able to stay together.

**Page 20**

**E. Comprehension Questions**  Listen and circle the correct answer.

1. Why does Mrs. Brown send her husband to the Adult Day-Care Center?
2. Why is Ann Ramos's daughter sending her to the Adult Day-Care Center?
3. Where do the patients in this program live?
4. When is the center open?
5. What is one activity that all the patients enjoy?
6. Why do some patients need physical therapy?
7. How does the Adult Day-Care Center help families to stay together?

## STRUCTURE

**Page 21**

**A. Present Tense**  Listen to these sentences. Write the present tense verb you hear.

1. David lives in a small apartment in the city.
2. His wife still works.
3. She leaves her husband alone during the day.
4. Ann Ramos lives with her daughter.
5. She follows her daughter all day.
6. Their families take them to the Adult Day-Care program.
7. Many hospitals offer this program.
8. The Center offers many activities.
9. Many patients like to cook.
10. Some patients need physical therapy.

## PRONUNCIATION

**Page 21**

**A. Linking with *-s***  Listen carefully and complete these sentences with the missing words. Mark the linking sounds.

When a final **-s** is followed by a vowel, the sounds are linked. The **-s** sounds like part of the next word.

Mr. Brown **participates in** the program.

1. David Brown lives at home.
2. He stays at home all day.
3. His wife works in an office.
4. She worries about her husband.
5. He forgets about little things in the house.
6. Ann Ramos participates in the program, too.
7. She needs a break.
8. She only goes in the morning.
9. Ann paints and plays cards with her friends.
10. The program offers activities for the elderly.

**Page 22**

**B. Is / Does**  Circle the answer to these questions. Listen carefully for *Is he, Is she, Does he,* or *Does she.*

We often do not hear the **h** in questions that begin with *Is* or *Does.*

Is he          Does he

1. Does he live in the city?
2. Is he forgetful?
3. Is he friendly?
4. Is she old?
5. Does she follow her daughter around?
6. Does she need a break?
7. Does he like to talk?
8. Is she busy?
9. Does she still work?
10. Is she worried about her husband?

**SPEAKERS**

**Page 22**

**Speaker 1**

I mainly stay at home and clean, and do housework and cook. And I love to read. I go to the library about once a week. I read books about history and politics. And I volunteer at the hospital two afternoons a week. I push around the cart from the gift store downstairs. It has newspapers and magazines and little things people want like perfume or powder or mouthwash. And once in a while I play cards with my friends.

**Speaker 2**

I still work part time. I had a butcher shop. My son owns it now, but I work there almost every morning. There are hobbies I enjoy, like reading and woodworking. I make furniture, especially tables and cabinets and shelves. I have a small woodshop downstairs in the basement and I spend two or three hours a day there.

**Speaker 3**

I'm 93 and thank goodness, I'm in good health. My son is 71. He had a stroke three years ago. And I go and I sit with him every afternoon until his wife comes home from work and then I go home. I love baseball. And he does too. I like this time of year because we watch baseball games on TV every afternoon. I know all the teams and players. And I read the sports section to my son, all about the teams and what's happening.

**Speaker 4**

I go to the gym and I take aerobics for people over 60. They give you exercises in the pool. That's three times a week. Seniors are far more active than they were ten or fifteen years ago. I went to my doctor and he said, "Get out and move." And so I do. I go to the pool and I walk about two miles a day. I'm not trying to lose weight, I just want to feel better and stay healthy.

**Speaker 5**

I belong to a senior citizens' center and I go there almost every day. We have book discussions and we talk about current events. We really know what's happening in the world. And once a week, we take the bus to a park. We sit under the trees or take short walks. It's just nice to get away from the city for a few hours. I don't drive anymore, a minivan picks me up at 9:00 and I'm home by about 2:00. And once in a while, we do something really special, like go to a show or to a concert. It's so important to get outside of yourself and stay interested and active.

**Speaker 6**

I live by myself and I can't get around too well. I'm 88 years old. I don't drive anymore. But I manage. A woman comes in every Tuesday and she cleans and takes me to the supermarket. I live in the same building that I had my children in. I've been here for about 50 years. And we all know one another. We visit with each other a lot and have each other over for tea or coffee or something sweet. And I watch a lot of TV. There's so many things it covers, it's wonderful for older people. And my son picks me up every Friday and I spend the weekend with him and his family in the suburbs.

## UNIT 4: Apartment Problems

**COMPREHENSION**

**Page 27**

**Story**

Theresa and Charles live in Chicago. They rent a one-bedroom apartment. Theresa is pregnant. She's expecting a baby in two months, so they're looking for a larger apartment.

Theresa and Charles are talking to the landlord in a large apartment building. He's showing them an apartment in his building. A family is living there now, but they're going to move next week. The landlord is also saying that there are a few problems in the apartment, but he's going to fix them.

Theresa and Charles are looking around the apartment. They can't believe the mess! In the kitchen, the oven door is open and the oven is smoking. Theresa is trying to open the refrigerator, but she can't. The door is stuck. And the heat isn't working, no hot air is coming up from the radiator.

Charles is in the bathroom. He can't see too well because the light isn't working. The sink is overflowing. Water is going all over the floor and Charles can't turn it off. And water is leaking from the ceiling. There's probably a problem in the apartment above this one.

Theresa and Charles aren't going to rent this apartment. They're leaving in a hurry!

**Page 28**

**E. Comprehension Questions**   Listen and circle the correct answer.

1. How big is Charles' and Theresa's apartment?
2. Why are they looking at apartments?
3. When is the family who is living in the apartment now going to move?
4. Why can't Theresa open the refrigerator door?
5. Why is water leaking from the ceiling?
6. Is the landlord going to fix all the problems?
7. Why are Theresa and Charles leaving in a hurry?

## STRUCTURE

**Page 29**

**A. Present Continuous Tense**   Listen to these sentences. Write the present continuous verb you hear.

1. Theresa is expecting a baby.
2. They're looking for a larger apartment.
3. Theresa and Charles are talking to the landlord.
4. A family of four is living here now.
5. The oven is smoking.
6. The heat isn't working.
7. No hot air is coming up from the radiator.
8. The sink is overflowing.
9. Water is leaking from the ceiling.
10. They're leaving in a hurry.

**Page 29**

**B. Tense Contrast**

Listen to these sentences. Decide if they are about now or the future. Circle *now* or *future*.

1. Theresa and Charles are looking at apartments.
2. They're going to look at several apartments today.
3. Theresa is pregnant.
4. A landlord is showing Theresa and Charles an apartment.

5. A family is living in this apartment.
6. They're going to move.
7. Nothing in this apartment is working.
8. The landlord isn't going to fix anything.
9. Theresa and Charles are leaving.
10. They aren't going to rent this apartment.

## PRONUNCIATION

**Page 29**

**A. Syllables**   Listen to these words. Write the number of syllables you hear on the line after each word.

| One syllable | Two syllables | Three syllables |
|---|---|---|
| week | landlord | apartment |
| door | baby | Chicago |
| light | building | probably |

1. live
2. larger
3. Theresa
4. air
5. ceiling
6. problem
7. expecting
8. leaking
9. smoking
10. family
11. around
12. stuck
13. rent
14. overflow
15. fix

**Page 30**

**B. Can / Can't**   Listen to these sentences. Write *can* or *can't* and the main verb.

> *Can* is pronounced *căn*. The main verb is stressed.
>    He căn sée.
> *Can't* is pronounced *cán't*. Usually, we don't hear the *t*. Both *can't* and the main verb are stressed.
>    He cán't sée.

1. They can't believe the mess.
2. He can't turn off the water.
3. She can't open the door.
4. He can't see too well.
5. They can look at other apartments.
6. They can stay in their apartment for another month.
7. They can't find an apartment they like.
8. They can call a real estate agency.
9. They can live with Theresa's family for a few months.
10. They can afford $500 rent; they can't afford $600.

## CONVERSATIONS

**Page 30**

**Conversation 1**

A: Jack Grimes here.
B: This is Mr. Wilcox, Apartment 427. Our toilet isn't working. It doesn't flush.
A: OK, Mr. Wilcox. I'll be up this morning at 10:00.
B: Thank you.

## Conversation 2

A: Jack Grimes here.

B: This is Mary Clark, Apartment 104. Mr. Grimes, there's water leaking into our kitchen. It's from the apartment above us.

A: How bad is the leak?

B: It's a small leak, but the ceiling is wet. I have a bucket under it.

A: OK. I'll be there on Wednesday.

## Conversation 3

A: Jack Grimes here.

B: Mr. Grimes, this is Sam Hadley, Apartment 346. The dishwasher isn't working.

A: I can get up later this week.

B: Later this week?

A: Yes, on Thursday or Friday.

## Conversation 4

A: Jack Grimes here.

B: This is Polly Selick, Apartment 634. I don't have any water.

A: No water?

B: Nothing. When I turn on the faucet, nothing comes out.

A: I'll take care of it tomorrow.

B: Tomorrow? I need you to take care of it today. I can't take a shower, I can't use the toilet, I can't cook.

A: OK. OK. I'll look at it this afternoon.

## Conversation 5

A: Jack Grimes here.

B: This is Bob Johnson, Apartment 402. Our refrigerator isn't working.

A: What's the problem?

B: I don't know. But it isn't cold. And all the food in the freezer defrosted.

A: I'll be up first thing tomorrow.

B: Tomorrow? What are we supposed to do for dinner tonight and breakfast tomorrow?

A: Well, I'll try to take care of it today.

## Conversation 6

A: Jack Grimes here.

B: Mr. Grimes, this is Ms. Davis, Apartment 315. We don't have any heat in our apartment. The radiators are cold.

A: I know. No one on your floor has heat. I called the plumber already. He's going to be here this afternoon.

B: I hope he's here early this afternoon. We're cold!

### Page 31

**C. Repeat the Last Word**    When people are upset, they often repeat the last word or phrase in a sentence. The intonation is the same as for a surprise or a question. Listen to these examples:

**Example 1:**    A: I'll be there tomorrow.
                   B: Tomorrow! I need you here today.

**Example 2:**    A: I'll fix it at 5:00.
                   B: At 5:00? But I don't have any water!

Now, listen to these sentences. Write the last word or phrase you hear.

1. I'll be there at 7:00.
2. I'll fix it tonight.
3. I can look at it next week.
4. I'll fix it first thing tomorrow.
5. I'll have a plumber there on Friday.
6. I can fix it on Tuesday.
7. I'll look at it this afternoon.
8. I'll see you tomorrow.
9. I'll be up in the morning.
10. I can check it on Monday.

# UNIT 5:  A Nation on the Move

### COMPREHENSION

**Page 35**

### Story

Every ten years the United States conducts a census of the population. A census is a count of the number of people who live in a city or a country. The government uses this information to get a better picture of its residents.

The last census was in 1990. In 1990, the population of the United States was about 250 million people. In 1980, ten years before that, the population was 227 million. That means the population is up 23 million people. This country is growing by about two million people a year.

The population map of the United States is changing. In the past, more people lived in the North and the Midwest. Now, these areas are staying the same in population or declining. Today, more people are living in the South and the West. These areas are growing.

Look at the numbers from the 1990 census. The population of New York City is up only 4%, the population of Boston is up just 2%. In Pennsylvania, the population of Pittsburgh is down 13%. In Michigan, the population of Detroit is down 2%.

At the same time, cities in the South and West are growing. In California, the population of San Jose is up 24% and Bakersfield is up 66%. In Texas, Austin is up 35% and San Antonio is up 19%. Nevada has the largest population increase of any state. Reno is up 33% and Las Vegas is up 57%. Florida continues to grow. For example, the population of Orlando is up 28%.

Why is the population map changing? The number one reason is jobs. Many large industries in the Northeast are closing or moving to the South or out of the country.

Also, in the past, there were thousands of small family farms in the Midwest. Now the farms are very large and machines do most of the work. Most new jobs are in the South and West. There's a need for builders, teachers, and store owners. The second reason that the South and West are growing is that the population is getting older. More people are retiring and they are choosing warm, sunny climates near the coast. Finally, many new immigrants are deciding to settle in the South and the West. For many, the climate is similar to that of their native countries and it is easier to find a job.

### Page 36

**E. Map Activity**   Look at the map at the bottom of page 34. Listen to this population information from the story. Indicate on the map how much the population of each city is up (+) or down (–). Look at New York City as an example.

1.  The population of New York City is up only 4%.
2.  The population of Boston is up just 2%.
3.  In Pennsylvania, the population of Pittsburgh is down 13%.
4.  In Michigan, the population of Detroit is down 2%.
5.  Florida continues to grow. For example, the population of Orlando is up 28%.
6.  In Texas, Austin is up 35% and San Antonio is up 19%.
7.  Nevada has the largest population increase of any state. Reno is up 33% and Las Vegas is up 57%.
8.  In California, the population of San Jose is up 24% and Bakersfield is up 66%.

### Page 36

**F. Comprehension Questions**   Listen and circle the correct answer.

1.  How often does the US. government conduct a census?
2.  In which city is the population growing?
3.  In which city is the population declining?
4.  In which direction are people moving?
5.  Why are there fewer jobs in the North?
6.  What is one reason that people are moving to the South?
7.  When will the government conduct the next census?

## STRUCTURE

### Page 37

**A. Present Continuous Tense**   Listen to these sentences. Write the present continuous verb you hear.

1.  Twenty-three million new residents are living in the United States.
2.  Some cities are growing in population.
3.  The population in some cities is staying the same.
4.  The South and West are growing.
5.  The population in the Northeast is declining.
6.  Many companies are closing.
7.  Some companies are moving to the South or West.

8.  Many older people are retiring to the South.
9.  They are choosing the sunny climate.
10. Many new immigrants are deciding to settle in the South and West.

## PRONUNCIATION

### Page 37

**A. Stressed Syllables**   Listen and mark the stressed syllable.

> In a two-syllable word, one syllable is stressed. It is longer and louder.
>
> a. condúct         c. pícture
> b. cénsus          d. todáy

| | | |
|---|---|---|
| 1. people | 6. reason | 11. country |
| 2. number | 7. decide | 12. decline |
| 3. retire | 8. before | 13. machine |
| 4. because | 9. moving | 14. teacher |
| 5. city | 10. million | 15. settle |

### Page 37

**B. Numbers**   This is a chart of the population of the United States from 1900 to 1990. Listen and complete the information. You will hear each sentence twice.

In 1900, the population of the United States was 76,100,000.

In 1910, the population of the United States was 92,400,000.

In 1920, the population of the United States was 106,500,000.

In 1930, the population of the United States was 123,100,000.

In 1940, the population of the United States was 132,500,000.

In 1950, the population of the United States was 152,300,000.

In 1960, the population of the United States was 180,700,000.

In 1970, the population of the United States was 205,100,000.

In 1980, the population of the United States was 227,700,000.

In 1990, the population of the United States was 249,900,000.

## CONVERSATIONS

### Page 38

### Conversation 1

A:  When you came to the United States, why did you settle in California?
B:  My brother lives here.
A:  How do you like it here?
B:  Well, I like the weather. But I can't find a job. I'm going to move to Nevada this summer.

**Conversation 2**

A: Why did you decide to live in Dallas?
B: I have a lot of friends here.
A: How do you like this area?
B: For me, I like it. I have a job and my kids like their school.
A: Are you going to stay here?
B: I sure am.

**Conversation 3**

A: How do you like Boston?
B: It's too cold.
A: Yeah, it is cold here.
B: When I finish school, I'm going to move to Arizona.
A: Why Arizona?
B: I have a cousin there.

**Conversation 4**

A: How do you like New York?
B: This is the city for me. I really like it here. There are restaurants, museums, and two baseball teams. There's always something to do.
A: Is your family here?
B: Yes, my brother and sister live here, too.

**Conversation 5**

A: Why did you decide to live in New Jersey?
B: Well, I was living in Pennsylvania, not in a city, but in a little town. But no one spoke Spanish there. I didn't feel comfortable.
A: Who told you about New Jersey?
B: A friend. She said that a lot of Spanish people live here. So, I moved and I really like it here.

**Conversation 6**

A: I hear you're retiring.
B: Yes, after 25 years at the company.
A: Are you going to stay here in Michigan?
B: It's too expensive here . . . and too cold. We're moving to Florida. We bought a nice house in a retirement community down there.

**Page 38**

**C. Why** If you want to know the reason that a speaker chose a specific place, item, time, etc., ask *Why* and the specific word. Use the article if the word is a singular noun. Listen to these examples.

**Example 1:** **A: I'm going to move to Arizona.**
**B: Why Arizona?**

**Example 2:** **A: I'm going to buy a Ford.**
**B: Why a Ford?**

Now, complete these questions.
1. I'm going to visit France.
2. I'm going to learn Japanese.

3. She's going to get married in November.
4. We're going to take Route 517.
5. They're going to paint the room red.
6. I'm going to buy a van.
7. He's going to get a police dog.
8. They're going to leave on Thursday.
9. She's going to move to Colorado.
10. They're going to take the train.

# UNIT 6: Jobs for the Future

## COMPREHENSION

**Page 43**

**Story**

Each year, the United States government publishes the *Occupational Outlook Handbook.* This large book lists over 250 kinds of jobs. It describes job duties, working conditions, education needed, and salary. Most importantly, it gives the job outlook. That is, it tells how many openings there will be for each job in the coming years. The job outlook may be excellent, good, or poor. This unit will look at the job outlook for seven jobs.

The job outlook for auto mechanics is good. The number of cars will continue to grow. Because cars are so expensive, people are keeping their cars longer. In the future, their cars will need more repairs.

Computer programmers will be in demand and the job outlook is excellent. There are more than 50 million computers in offices and homes in the United States. Both companies and individuals depend on computers for information, record keeping, and services.

The men and women who deliver the mail every day face a poor job future. Companies will use computers and fax machines to send information. And people will buy their stamps at supermarkets and department stores.

The job outlook for nurses is excellent. The population is increasing and people are living longer. Most jobs will open in large city hospitals and in country areas.

The outlook for travel agents is excellent. As incomes rise, people will take more vacations. Many couples, especially older couples, are taking two vacations a year. Charter flights, tours, and lower air fares will encourage more people to travel.

Because of the concern about safety and crime, one of the fastest growing jobs in the country is security guard. Guards are needed in prisons, but now they are also present in airports, stores, government buildings, and at sports events. Finally, the job outlook for teachers is good. The school age population is increasing, especially in the South and West. Many teachers are in their forties and fifties and will retire in the next ten years.

The *Occupational Outlook Handbook* is in the reference section of the library. It can tell you if the work you are interested in has a future or not.

**Page 44**

**E. Comprehension Questions**   Listen and circle the correct answer.

1. What does the *Occupational Outlook Handbook* describe?
2. The job outlook for mail carriers is poor. What does that mean?
3. Computer programmers will be in demand. What does that mean?
4. Why is the job outlook for auto mechanics good?
5. Why is the outlook for travel agents excellent?
6. Where will a teacher have a better opportunity to find a job?
7. Which job has the best job outlook?

## STRUCTURE

**Page 45**

**A. Future Tense**   Listen to these sentences. Write the future verb you hear.

1. There will be many new jobs.
2. Cars will need more repairs.
3. Companies will send information by fax.
4. People will buy their stamps at the supermarket.
5. Most nursing jobs will open in big cities.
6. People will take more vacations.
7. Companies will continue to move overseas.
8. Customers will use automated services.
9. Lower air fares will encourage people to fly.
10. Many teachers will retire.

**Page 45**

**B. Tense Contrast**   Listen to these sentences. Decide if they are about now or the future. Circle *now* or *future*.

1. People are keeping their cars longer.
2. Their cars will need more repairs.
3. Companies will use fax machines to send information.
4. People are living longer.
5. Jobs for nurses will open in city hospitals.
6. People will take more vacations.
7. Many older people are taking two vacations a year.
8. Lower airfares will encourage people to travel.
9. The school age population is increasing.
10. Many teachers will retire.

## PRONUNCIATION

**Page 45**

**A. Stressed Syllables**   Listen and mark the stressed syllable.

> In a three-syllable word, one syllable is stressed. It is longer and louder.
>
> a. impórtant      c. expénsive
> b. góvernment     d. cómpany

1. services
2. United
3. deliver
4. customer
5. offices
6. computer
7. condition
8. registered
9. overseas
10. practical
11. openings
12. excellent
13. continue
14. vacation
15. hospital

**Page 46**

**B. Numbers**   This is a list of the average yearly salary for ten jobs. Listen and complete the information. You will hear each sentence twice.

1. The average yearly salary for an auto mechanic is between $28,000 and $36,000.
2. The average yearly salary for a computer programmer is between $32,000 and $44,000.
3. The average yearly salary for a mail carrier is about $29,000.
4. The average yearly salary for a licensed practical nurse is between $17,000 and $22,000.
5. The average yearly salary for a registered nurse is between $27,000 and $33,000.
6. The average yearly salary for a travel agent is between $18,000 and $22,000.
7. The average yearly salary for a guard is about $19,000.
8. The average yearly salary for a police officer is about $29,000.
9. The average yearly salary for an elementary school teacher is about $32,000.
10. The average yearly salary for a secondary school teacher is about $34,000.

## CONVERSATIONS

**Page 46**

### Conversation 1
A: Business is really slow.
B: Yeah?
A: My company laid off three more people last week.
B: In your department?
A: Yeah. I hope I'm not the next.

### Conversation 2
A: How's your new job?
B: I like it.
A: What do you do?
B: I just stand at the door and check ID cards.

### Conversation 3
A: I have lots of free time now. I'm on unemployment.
B: What happened?
A: My company moved to Korea. Everybody got laid off.

### Conversation 4
A: I'm taking a computer course.
B: How come? Did you lose your job?
A: No, but my boss is 68 or 69 years old. I think he'll retire in a year or two. Then, I don't know what's going to happen.
B: So, you want to be ready.

### Conversation 5

A: I fill out one or two job applications a week, but no one is hiring.

B: I hear they're looking for school bus drivers at the Yellow Bus Company.

A: Oh, yeah? Do you know what they're paying?

B: My cousin works there. I think they pay about nine dollars an hour.

A: Thanks. I'll look into it.

### Conversation 6

A: My company hired 15 new workers last year.

B: What kind of company is that?

A: It's a home health care company. We work with the elderly and with people who just came out of the hospital, you know, like after an operation or a heart attack.

B: Why did you need so many people?

A: Well, there are a lot more older people. And we have a good reputation. People know we give really good care.

**Page 47**

**C. Same or Different**  Read each sentence. Then, listen and decide if the meaning is the same or different. Circle *S* or *D*.

1. My company let three more people go last week.
2. I hope I'm not the next.
3. How's your new job?
4. How come?
5. You want to be ready.
6. I'll look into that.
7. We have a good reputation.

## UNIT 7: Drunk Driver

### COMPREHENSION

**Page 51**

### Story

It's the beginning of a holiday weekend. Police officer Ed Williams and ten other officers are receiving instructions from their captain. They're on a special watch this weekend, trying to prevent accidents by drunk drivers. This weekend, over 400 people in the United States are going to die from accidents caused by drunk drivers. Over 4,000 people are going to receive serious injuries, all caused by drunk drivers.

At the same time, Joe Frazier is enjoying himself at a family party. He's been there for four hours. It's getting late and he's telling his sister that he's going to leave. She's asking him to stay and sleep over. But he thinks he can drive safely. "Don't worry. I'm going to be fine. I'm going to drive slowly. I only had a few drinks."

Officer Williams is in a parking lot, watching cars on the main street. A white car is coming toward him, weaving from left to right. Officer Williams stops the car

and tells Joe to get out. He asks Joe to walk along the white line. He can't do it. Officer Williams arrests Joe and takes him to the police station. At the police station, Joe fails the breath test. Officer Williams issues him a summons. Joe calls his sister. She's going to post $350 bail and drive him to her house.

This is Joe's first offense. He's going to appear in court next week. According to the law in his state, Joe is going to receive a $400 fine. The judge is going to suspend his license for six months. Also, Joe has to attend a special program for drunk drivers and do community service. Joe knows, too, that his insurance is going to go up an additional $1,000 a year for three years. Joe is angry at himself. He was stupid to drive. He's worried about the extra money and how he's going to get to work. He will never drink and drive again.

**Page 52**

**E. Comprehension Questions**  Listen and circle the correct answer.

1. Why is this weekend special?
2. How many people are going to die in accidents this weekend?
3. What does Joe's sister want him to do?
4. Where does Officer Williams stop Joe?
5. Why does he stop Joe's car?
6. What can't Joe do?
7. How is Joe going to get to work for the next six months?

### STRUCTURE

**Page 53**

**A. Future Tense**  Listen to these sentences. Write the future verb you hear. In spoken English, *going to* sounds like *gonna*.

1. Joe is going to drive home.
2. He's going to leave.
3. I'm going to drive slowly.
4. His sister is going to post bail.
5. She's going to drive him home.
6. He's going to appear in court next week.
7. Joe is going to pay a $400 fine.
8. The judge is going to suspend his license.
9. He's going to attend a special program.
10. His insurance is going to go up.

### PRONUNCIATION

**Page 53**

**A. *His / Him***  Listen carefully and complete these sentences with *his* or *him*.

> We hear the ***h*** in *his* and *him* when it is the first word in a sentence. We often don't hear the ***h*** in *his* and *him* when it follows another word.
>
> *His* often sounds like *ħis*. — He's at ħis sister's house.
> *Him* often sounds like *ħim*. — She's talking to ħim.

1. He's talking to his sister.
2. She's asking him to stay.
3. The officer arrested him.
4. They took him to the police station.
5. The officer is going to issue him a summons.
6. Joe's going to call his sister.
7. She's going to drive him to her house.
8. He can't drive his car home.
9. They're going to fine him $400.
10. He's going to lose his license.

**Page 54**

**B. Stressed Words**   Listen and complete these sentences with the stressed words.

> In speaking, the important words in a sentence are stressed. They are longer and louder. These are the content words (nouns, verbs, adjectives, and adverbs).

1. It's a holiday weekend.
2. Joe is at a party.
3. He's going to leave.
4. She's asking him to stay.
5. I'm going to be fine.
6. I'm going to drive slowly.
7. The officer is going to take him to the police station.
8. His sister is going to drive him to her house.
9. The judge is going to suspend his license.
10. He was stupid to drink and drive.

## CONVERSATIONS

**Page 54**

### Conversation 1

J:  The charge is MV132. Driving without vehicle registration or insurance.
D:  I have the papers.
J:  These weren't in the vehicle?
D:  No.
J:  When you drive a vehicle, you're supposed to have these with you.
D:  I know. But I was driving the company truck.
J:  It's your responsibility to be sure they're in the truck. The fine is $20 plus $15 court costs. And the same problem with the registration?
D:  Yes.
J:  That's an additional $20 and $15 court costs.

### Conversation 2

J:  MV144. The charge is failure to stop at a stop sign. How do you plead?
D:  Guilty.
J:  Is there anything you want to say?
D:  No.
J:  There was an accident involved?
D:  Yes.

J:  Was anyone hurt?
D:  No.
J:  The other driver was a Ms. Hunter. How do you know she wasn't hurt?
D:  She was walking around after the accident.
J:  No emergency vehicles came?
D:  No.
J:  The fine is $70 plus $20 court costs.

### Conversation 3

J:  MV199. Failure to stop at a red light. Do you understand the charge?
D:  Yes.
J:  How do you plead?
D:  Guilty.
J:  Was there an accident?
D:  Yes.
J:  How many vehicles were involved in the accident?
D:  Three!?
J:  Was anyone hurt? Injured?
D:  No.
J:  Did any emergency vehicles come?
D:  No.
J:  The fine is $100 plus $20 court costs.

### Conversation 4

J:  M1332. The charge is driving without a license and you failed to appear in court. How do you plead?
D:  Guilty.
J:  The fine is $25. And you also got a failure to appear notice. That's $60. Court costs, $20. That's a total due of $105.

### Conversation 5

J:  MV107.  Speeding. You were driving 40 miles per hour in a 25 mile per hour zone. How do you plead?
D:  Guilty. With an explanation.
J:  Yes?
D:  I wasn't speeding. I was driving 25 miles per hour. But there was a car in front of me, only going 15 or 20. I think he was looking for someone's address. I finally passed him. And it was just at that moment that the police officer saw me.
J:  You were going 40 miles an hour. The speed limit was 25. The fine is $50 plus $15 court costs.

### Conversation 6

J:  MV172.  Failure to stop for a school bus. How do you plead?
D:  Guilty.
J:  Mr. Jenkins, this is a very serious offense.
D:  Yes, sir.
J:  You have an explanation?
D:  No, sir. I guess I wasn't paying attention.
J:  I guess you need to pay a lot more attention when you're driving. The fine is $200 plus $25 court costs.

Page 55

**C. Question Intonation**   This judge asked several questions. At times, he used a question with question intonation. At other times, he used a statement with question intonation. Listen to the intonation of these sentences. Put a period if you hear a statement. Put a question mark if you hear a question.

> **Examples:**
> **There was an accident.**
> **Was there an accident?**
> **There was an accident?**

1. There was an accident?
2. You were driving 40 miles per hour.
3. No emergency vehicles came?
4. They weren't in the vehicle?
5. The fine is $40.
6. This summons was issued on March 10th.
7. And the same problem with the registration?
8. This is a very serious offense.
9. You understand the charge?
10. You have an explanation?

# UNIT 8:  A Professional

## COMPREHENSION

Page 59

### Story

Richard Williams works hard. He's intelligent, careful, and fast. His work is dangerous. Richard thinks of himself as a professional, a professional thief.

Yesterday was a typical day. Richard dressed in a business suit, took his briefcase, and drove to a town about ten miles from his home. He parked his car in a busy area, then began to walk along the street. He was just another businessman, walking to work.

At 8:00, Richard saw what he wanted. A man was leaving his house. Richard walked around the block again. At 8:05, he watched a woman leave the same house. After she left, Richard worked quickly. He walked to the side of the house and stood behind a tree. He took a screwdriver out of his briefcase and quickly opened the window and climbed in. First, he looked through the desk in the living room. He found $500 in cash. In the dining room, he put the silverware into his briefcase. The next stop was the bedroom. Richard stole a diamond ring and an emerald necklace. He also took a camera. Richard passed a color TV, a stereo, and a computer, but he didn't touch them. Everything had to fit into his briefcase. In less than five minutes, Richard climbed back out the window. He looked around carefully, then began his walk down the street again. No one looked at him. He was just another businessman, walking to work.

Page 60

**E. Comprehension Questions**   Listen and circle the correct answer.

1. Why did Richard wear a business suit?
2. What did Richard do after the man left his house?
3. Why didn't anyone see Richard get into the house?
4. Why didn't Richard take the television set?
5. How long did Richard stay in the house?
6. What did Richard steal?
7. What kind of weather is best for Richard's work?

## STRUCTURE

Page 61

**A. Past Tense**   Listen to these sentences. Write the past tense verb you hear.

1. Richard dressed in a business suit.
2. He parked his car in a busy area.
3. He walked around the block.
4. He watched a woman leave her house.
5. Richard worked quickly.
6. He opened the window.
7. He climbed in.
8. He looked through the desk.
9. Richard passed a computer.
10. He climbed back out the window.

Page 61

**B. Tense Contrast**   Listen to these sentences. Decide the tense of the verb. Circle *present*, *past*, or *future*.

1. Richard works hard.
2. He stole $500 in cash.
3. He's going to sell the camera for $200.
4. He always wears a business suit.
5. He wears gloves so that he doesn't leave fingerprints.
6. Last week, he robbed eight homes.
7. He made over $3,000.
8. Richard works alone.
9. Richard doesn't enter homes with security systems.
10. Someday, the police are going to catch him.

## PRONUNCIATION

Page 61

**A. -ed Endings**   Say each of these past tense verbs to yourself. Decide if it has one or two syllables. Then, listen to the pronunciation of each verb. Write the number of syllables you hear.

1. parked
2. wanted
3. dressed
4. worked
5. needed
6. said
7. climbed
8. waited
9. walked
10. started
11. robbed
12. carried
13. hated
14. arrived

**Page 62**

**B. Linking with -ed**   Listen carefully and complete these sentences with the missing words. Mark the linking sounds.

> When a final **-ed** is followed by a vowel, the sounds are linked. The **-d** sounds like part of the next word.
>
> He watche**d a** woman leave the house.

1. He parked on Main Street.
2. He dressed in a business suit.
3. He walked around the block.
4. He passed a color TV.
5. He worked in the morning.
6. He carried a briefcase.
7. He opened a window.
8. He climbed in.
9. He arrived at 8:15.
10. He robbed a house every day.

**Page 62**

**C. Stressed Words**   Listen and complete these sentences with the stressed words.

> In speaking, the important words in a sentence are stressed. They are longer and louder. These are the content words (nouns, verbs, adjectives, and adverbs).
>
> He **stóle** a **ríng** and a **nécklace.**

1. Richard works hard.
2. His work is dangerous.
3. He drove to a town about ten miles from his home.
4. He parked his car in a busy area.
5. A man was leaving his house.
6. Richard walked to the side of the house.
7. He took a screwdriver out of his briefcase.
8. He opened the window and climbed in.
9. He looked through the desk in the living room.
10. He found $500 in cash.

## CONVERSATIONS

**Page 63**

### Conversation 1

The first conversation is on Monday. It is between the police officer and Mr. and Mrs. Jackson, the couple in the story.

| | |
|---|---|
| Officer: | Mr. Jackson, we just checked around the house. The thief got in through the side window. |
| Mr. Jackson: | The side window? |
| Officer: | Yes, we found footprints under the window and there's dirt on the carpet inside, in the living room. And there are marks on the window outside. He probably used a screwdriver to open the window. Now, what did he take? |
| Mr. Jackson: | Our cash. We had about $500 in the desk. |
| Mrs. Jackson: | And he took my jewelry. My diamond ring and emerald necklace are gone. And he stole the silverware. |
| Mr. Jackson: | He took my camera, too. It was a brand new camera, I only used it once. |
| Mrs. Jackson: | Why didn't he take the computer or the television set? |
| Officer: | He was on foot. He only took what he could carry. |

### Conversation 2

The second conversation is on Tuesday. It is between Danielle Smith and the same police officer.

| | |
|---|---|
| Officer: | What happened? |
| Danielle: | Well, I left for work at about 8:30, but when I got to the light, I saw I forgot my briefcase, so I drove back home. And when I drove in the driveway, I saw a man run out the front door. |
| Officer: | Which way did he go? |
| Danielle: | He ran up the street and he jumped into a car, it was a black car, and he drove away fast. |
| Officer: | Did you get the license plate number? |
| Danielle: | No, he was too far away. But the car was new. It was a . . . it was a new Ford. A Mustang. |
| Officer: | Did you get a good look at him? |
| Danielle: | No, not really. He was tall and thin. He was white and he had brown hair. And he was wearing a business suit. |
| Officer: | Did he take anything? |
| Danielle: | I don't think he had time to take anything. I think I surprised him. |

### Conversation 3

The third conversation is on Wednesday. It is between Arthur Manley and the same police officer.

| | |
|---|---|
| Officer: | What happened? |
| Arthur: | Well, my brother and his wife left for work at 7:30. A few minutes later, somebody got into the house. I guess he thought the house was empty. |
| Officer: | Where were you? |
| Arthur: | I was still in bed. I heard something in the living room, so I went downstairs. And there was this man, putting money into his briefcase. I guess I surprised him. He ran out the front door and I ran after him. |
| Officer: | It's good he didn't have a gun. |
| Arthur: | You said it! Well, he fell down the steps and broke his leg. That's when I called you. |
| Officer: | We've been looking for this man. In the past two weeks, he broke into 20 homes in this area. |

**Page 63**

**A. Three Robberies**   Look at the pictures and listen to these three conversations between a police officer and three families that Richard robbed. Then, listen to sentences from the conversations. Do they refer to Conversation A, B, or C? Circle the correct conversation.

1. I forgot my briefcase, so I drove back home.
2. We found footprints under the window.
3. I heard something in the living room, so I went downstairs.
4. He took my jewelry.
5. He ran out the front door and I ran after him.
6. We had about $500 in the desk.
7. He fell down the stairs and broke his leg.
8. He ran up the street and he jumped into a car.

**Page 64**

**C. Same or Different**   Read each sentence. Then, listen and decide if the meaning is the same or different. Circle S or D.

1. My diamond ring is gone.
2. Which way did he go?
3. Did you get the license plate number?
4. Did you get a good look at him?
5. I surprised him.
6. He thought the house was empty.
7. You said it!
8. He broke into 20 homes.

**Page 64**

**D. Questions with *Did***   Listen to these questions about the robberies. Complete them with *Did he*, *Did she*, or *Did you*.

> **Examples:**
> **Did he climb in the window?**
> **Did she run after the thief?**
> **Did you get the license plate number?**

1. Did he take anything?
2. Did you get his license?
3. Did she surprise him?
4. Did he have a gun?
5. Did he break the window?
6. Did you get a good look at him?
7. Did she call the police?
8. Did you hear something downstairs?
9. Did you run after him?
10. Did he say anything to you?

# UNIT 9:  The Lottery

## COMPREHENSION

**Page 69**

### Story

Did you ever dream of winning the lottery? So have millions of other people. Every day, millions of Americans buy lottery tickets. They are hoping to win $50,000, $100,000, one million dollars or more.

When a person wins a million dollars, he doesn't receive a check for the total amount. The person receives $50,000 a year for 20 years. Also, he must pay taxes. After taxes, a million-dollar winner receives from $25,000 to $40,000 a year for 20 years.

What have some people done with their money? Let's look at four past winners. Lisa K. wanted to be an artist, but she didn't have enough money to go to school. She was working as a cashier in a supermarket. In August, Lisa bought one ticket and won two million dollars. She quit her job and is now attending art school. Lisa says, "If I don't become an artist, it's my own fault. I have the opportunity now."

Mark L. was a car salesperson. He worked seven days a week and had little time for family life. After he won three million dollars, he quit working. Now he spends his time bowling, working in the garden, and fixing things in his house. But, he's bored. He doesn't want to sell cars again, but he isn't sure what he wants to do with his life.

Mabel S. was over 60 years old and retired when she won a million dollars. She started to spend her money immediately. She bought a new car, new clothes, and new furniture for her house. She paid for her son's college tuition and bought a car for him, too. Then she gave all her grandchildren money. After a few months, she had no money left to pay her bills. Also, she forgot about taxes and didn't have enough money to pay them. She plans to spend her money more carefully next year.

Jack B.'s winning ticket was worth two million dollars. He is one of the small number of winners who did not quit his job. Jack still teaches English at a high school in his area. But he and his wife now have a new car in the garage. They take their four children on an interesting vacation every year. And they don't worry about sending their children to college. They say that money brings security and gives a person opportunities, but it doesn't bring happiness.

**Page 70**

**E. Comprehension Questions**   Listen and circle the correct answer.

1. How many people buy lottery tickets every day?
2. After taxes, how much does a million-dollar lottery winner receive each year?
3. What did most of the winners do after they won the lottery?
4. What is Lisa's dream?
5. Mark quit his job and has lots of money. Why isn't he happy?
6. What's Mabel going to do with her money next year?
7. According to Jack and his wife, what does money bring?

## STRUCTURE

**Page 71**

**A. Past Irregular Verbs**   Listen to these sentences. Write the verb you hear.

1. Lisa bought one lottery ticket.
2. She won two million dollars.
3. She quit her job.
4. Mark was a car salesperson.
5. He had little time for family life.
6. Mabel spent money on her family.
7. She bought a new car.
8. She paid for her son's college tuition.
9. She gave money to her grandchildren.
10. She forgot about her taxes.

**Page 71**

**B. Negatives**   Listen to these sentences. Circle the negative verb you hear.

1. Jack didn't quit his job.
2. He doesn't worry about sending his children to college.
3. Lisa didn't enjoy her job.
4. If she doesn't become an artist, it's her own fault.
5. She didn't have the opportunity before this.
6. Mark doesn't know what to do with his time.
7. He didn't have time for his family.
8. He doesn't want to sell cars again.
9. Mabel didn't spend her money carefully.
10. She didn't have enough money to pay her taxes.

## PRONUNCIATION

**Page 72**

**A. Linking with A / An**   Complete these sentences with the missing words. Mark the linking sounds.

> When a final consonant is followed by **a** or **an,** the sounds are linked. **A** or **an** sounds like part of the word before.
>    He **won a** million dollars.

1. When a person wins a million dollars, he must pay taxes.
2. He doesn't receive a check for the total amount.
3. She was a cashier.
4. She wants to become an artist.
5. Mark was a car salesman.
6. He worked seven days a week.
7. She won a million dollars.
8. She bought a new car.
9. He teaches at a high school.
10. Money gives a person opportunities.

**Page 72**

**B. *Did he / Does he***   *Did he* and *Does he* can sound similar. Listen and complete these questions with *Did he* or *Does he.*

> We often do not hear the sound of the **h** after *did* or *does.*
>
> Did he like his job?      Does he like his job?

1. Did he buy a ticket?
2. Does he work now?
3. Did he like his job?
4. Does he work at home now?
5. Does he know what he wants to do?
6. Did he win two million dollars?
7. Did he quit his job?
8. Does he still teach English?
9. Does he have a new car?
10. Does he worry about money?

## CONVERSATIONS

**Page 73**

### Conversation 1

A: Do you ever buy lottery tickets?
B: Yeah, every week, I try the Pick-6. This week, it's up to four million dollars.
A: How much do you spend on tickets?
B: Spend? You mean waste. I buy five tickets a week, five dollars. And I never win a penny. But I still keep buying tickets.

### Conversation 2

A: Do you ever buy lottery tickets?
B: Yup. I get paid on Friday. And on the way home, I buy two or three.
A: What numbers do you play?
B: Well, on one ticket, I always play the same number. I put my birthday, my wife's birthday and the kids' birthdays. For the other tickets, I just let the machine pick the numbers, you know, the Quick Pick.

### Conversation 3

A: Do you ever buy lottery tickets?
B: Me, no. But my cousin won the lottery about two years ago.
A: Really?
B: Really. He bought a house with the money. A beautiful big house with four bedrooms and a great kitchen.
A: Did he quit work?
B: No. The money pays the mortgage and taxes and things for the house, but they still have to eat.

### Conversation 4

A: Do you ever buy lottery tickets?
B: Well, sometimes. Like if the jackpot is really big, say over ten million, then I buy one or two.

### Conversation 5

A: Do you ever buy lottery tickets?
B: I used to. Every week, I bought three. And I did that for about six or seven years. And I never won a penny. And so one day I stopped. I never bought another ticket.

## Conversation 6

A: Do you ever buy lottery tickets?

B: Sure, I spend about $10 dollars a week on tickets. I buy the Pick 3's and the Pick 4's.

A: Did you ever win any money?

B: Yes, a couple of times. Once I won $630 and another time I won almost $2,000.

## Conversation 7

A: Do you ever buy lottery tickets?

B: Yup. One a week. I know it's not a lot, but someone's going to win that money and someday, it's going to be me.

### Page 73

**C. Same or Different**   Read each sentence. Then, listen and decide if the meaning is the same or different. Circle S or D.

1. I never win a penny.
2. I still keep buying tickets.
3. They still have to eat.
4. I used to buy lottery tickets.
5. I never bought another ticket.
6. Someday it's going to be me.
7. I buy tickets on the way home.

# UNIT 10: Marco Polo

## COMPREHENSION

### Page 77

### Story

The most famous traveler in all of history was Marco Polo. He was one of the first Europeans to visit China and the Far East. At the age of 17, he left Italy with his father and uncle. It took them more than three years to cross the mountains and deserts of Asia. In the year 1275, they reached China and the palace of Kublai Khan, the great emperor. They stayed in China for almost 20 years, as guests of the emperor. He sent them on many trips around his empire. They were amazed at what they saw. China was a country far more advanced than Italy or any other country in Europe.

After he returned to Italy, Marco Polo dictated many of his stories to a friend. His book, *Description of the World,* became the most popular book in Europe. People found it difficult to believe his stories of people, animals, places, and things. They were so different from Europe at that time. These are a few of Marco Polo's descriptions.

In one area of China, there were black stones. People dug them out of the mountains. They lit the black stones and they burned very slowly, giving off heat. The people used these stones to cook and heat their homes.

In China there was a great system of highways. These highways had two lanes paved with stone or brick. Men planted trees every ten feet to keep the sun off of travelers' heads.

The Chinese people were also very clean. In every town, there were many public baths. Everyone bathed at least three times a week. Rich families built baths in their homes and bathed daily.

China was one of the first countries to use paper money. The government made bills from the bark of a special tree. They signed the money and stamped it with the royal seal. The people could use this money the same as they could use gold or silver.

On one of his trips in the south of China, Marco saw a strange animal which lived along the rivers. The crocodile looked like a large piece of wood and was more than ten feet long. In the front, it had two small legs. Its eyes were very large. Its mouth was big enough to eat a man and its teeth were long and sharp.

Most people believed Marco Polo's stories. But others told him they didn't believe his descriptions. He answered that he didn't tell half of what he saw.

### Page 79

**E. Comprehension Questions**   Listen and circle the correct answer.

1. What country was Marco Polo from?
2. Did he travel alone?
3. How long did Marco Polo stay in China?
4. How did people in China heat their homes in 1275?
5. Why were Europeans amazed that China had paved highways?
6. What animal did Marco Polo see in the south of China?
7. Did everyone believe Marco Polo's stories?

## STRUCTURE

### Page 79

**A. Past Irregular Tense**   Listen to these sentences. Write the past tense verb you hear.

1. Marco Polo left Italy with his father and uncle.
2. It took them more than three years to reach China.
3. The emperor sent them on many trips around his empire.
4. *Description of the World* became the most popular book in Europe.
5. People dug black stones out of the mountains.
6. They lit them.
7. The highways had two lanes.
8. Rich families built baths in their homes.
9. The government made bills from the bark of a special tree.
10. Marco saw a strange animal in the south of China.

### Page 80

**B. *One of the* + adjective**   Listen and complete these sentences with *one of the* and the adjective.

> In *one of the,* the words are linked. We usually don't hear the **f** in *of.*
>
> Kublai Khan was **one of the** most powerful emperors of China.

1. Marco Polo was one of the most famous travelers of all times.
2. He was one of the first Europeans to visit China.
3. China was one of the most advanced countries in the world.
4. Kublai Khan was one of the greatest emperors of China.
5. *Description of the World* became one of the most popular books in Europe.
6. China had one of the most efficient highway systems in the world.
7. It was one of the first countries to use paper money.
8. The crocodile was one of the strangest animals that Marco Polo ever saw.

## PRONUNCIATION

**Page 80**

**A. *Was / Were*** Listen to these sentences. Circle *was* or *were*.

1. China was an advanced country.
2. In one area, there were black stones.
3. There was a great system of highways.
4. There were trees every ten feet.
5. The Chinese people were very clean.
6. There were public baths in every town.
7. China was one of the first countries to use paper money.
8. There was a strange animal in the river.
9. It was more than ten feet long.
10. Its teeth were very sharp.

**Page 81**

**B. Linking with *-ed*** Listen carefully and complete these sentences with the missing words. Mark the linking sounds.

> When a final *-ed* is followed by a vowel, the sounds are linked. The *-d* sounds like part of the next word.
> People were surprise**d at** his stories.

1. Marco Polo and his father stayed in China for 20 years.
2. They lived at the palace of the emperor.
3. They traveled around China for many years.
4. The Chinese bathed at least three times a week.
5. They stamped it with the royal seal.
6. Marco Polo looked at the strange animal in the river.
7. The Polos crossed Asia by horse and camel.
8. Marco Polo talked about his travels with a friend.
9. Some people believed all his stories.
10. Everyone was amazed at his stories of China.

## CONVERSATIONS

**Page 81**

### Conversation 1

A: This machine drives me crazy.
B: How come?
A: Well, most of the time, it's fine. I rent a movie and I put it in and press ON. But the other day, I wanted to program it, like, to record a show. So, I read the directions. And I followed them exactly, you know, step by step, but then, nothing. It didn't record.
B: Is there something wrong with the machine?
A: With the machine? No. There's something wrong with me. I'm no good with, like, electronic equipment.

### Conversation 2

A: My dad's talking about getting one of those video phones, you know, the kind that you can see the person you're talking to and they can see you.
B: Oh, I'd hate that.
A: Yeah, I think it's a crazy idea. I mean, I'd feel uncomfortable.
B: Right, the phone would ring and you'd think, "I have to comb my hair before I answer the phone".

### Conversation 3

A: I just got a computer.
B: Oh. What kind?
A: A Dynamax.
B: That's great. You can do your homework and your reports on it.
A: And it's right in my room. I don't have to go to the computer lab and, like, wait for one to be free.

### Conversation 4

A: Do you have a fax machine at home?
B: At home? No!
A: Well, this week, two times, someone asked if I had a fax machine. They wanted to send me information through the telephone.
B: Who asked you?
A: Well, I'm buying a car. The first was the bank. They wanted to fax me a loan application. And the other was a car dealer. They wanted to fax me some information on a new car.
B: I guess I'm behind the times. I'm still using the mail.

### Conversation 5

A: I don't need to go to the bank anymore.
B: Me neither. Maybe just once a month.
A: I used to go once or twice a week. But now, the company I work for, they deposit our paychecks in our bank accounts automatically. And when I need cash, I use one of the automatic teller machines. I mean, they're everywhere!
B: Well, I just put everything on my credit card. My problem is paying it off at the end of the month.

### Conversation 6

A: Did you ever see one of these? It's a Spanish-English dictionary, but it's a machine.
B: How does it work?
A: Look. You just type in a word in Spanish. Like, I'll type casa, c-a-s-a. And then you press ENTER. And, look, you see the word in English. See, house, h-o-u-s-e.

B: That's great! You know, I think I'll get my mother one of these for her birthday.

**Page 82**

**B. Meaning**  Listen to each sentence. Circle the letter of the sentence with the same meaning.

1. How come?
2. Is there something wrong with the machine?
3. I'm no good with electronic equipment.
4. My dad is talking about getting one of those video phones.
5. I think it's a crazy idea.
6. I'm still using the mail.
7. Me neither.
8. I used to go to the bank once or twice a week.

**Page 82**

**C. Conversation Fillers (Well / I mean / Like / You know)**  In informal conversation, people often use conversation fillers. Some people, especially young people, use fillers in almost every sentence. These words have no meaning. They give the speaker time to pause and then continue the conversation. Common fillers are *Well, I mean, like,* and *you know.* Listen to these sentences and circle the fillers you hear.

1. Well, most of the time, it's fine.
2. I wanted to program it, like, to record a show.
3. And I followed them exactly, you know, step by step.
4. My dad's talking about getting one of those video phones, you know, the kind that you can see the person you're talking to and they can see you.
5. I mean, I'd feel uncomfortable.
6. I don't have to go to the computer lab and, like, wait for one to be free.
7. Well, I'm buying a car.
8. I mean, they're everywhere.
9. Well, I just put everything on my credit card.
10. You know, I think I'll get my mother one of these for her birthday.

# UNIT 11:  Can I Borrow a Dollar?

## COMPREHENSION

**Page 87**

**Story**

Hoang is a college student. He needed a part-time job to pay for the bus, his books, and clothes. Last month he found a job at Video World. Several other young people work there in the evening and on Saturday and Sunday. Hoang became friendly with all of them, especially Steve.

The first week of work, Steve said, "I'd like a soda. Do you have seventy-five cents?" Hoang said, "Sure."

The second week of work, Steve and Hoang had their lunch break together. They went across the street and ordered hamburgers, french fries, and sodas. When the bill came, Steve asked, "Can I borrow five dollars? I'll pay you

back tomorrow." Hoang said, "No problem." But Steve never paid him back.

The third week, as Steve and Hoang were leaving work, Steve said, "I need gas to get home, but I forgot my wallet. Could you lend me ten dollars until tomorrow?" Hoang said, "Well, OK," but he never saw his ten dollars again.

Yesterday, Steve asked Hoang, "Can I borrow twelve dollars? I told my Mom I'd get a haircut, but I didn't take any money." "Sorry," Hoang said. "I'm broke."

**Page 88**

**E. Listen and Decide**  Listen to Steve's requests. Circle Hoang's response.

1. Can I borrow 75¢ for a soda?
2. Can I borrow $5.00 for lunch?
3. Could you lend me $10 for gas?
4. Can you lend me $12 for a haircut?

## STRUCTURE

**Page 88**

**A. Requests**  Listen to these requests. Each starts with *Can I, Can you, Could I,* or *Could you.* Write the sentences you hear. You will hear each sentence twice.

1. Can I borrow ten dollars?
2. Could I borrow a dollar?
3. Could you lend me five dollars?
4. Can you lend me twenty dollars?
5. Can I borrow a quarter?
6. Could you lend me two dollars?
7. Can I borrow fifty cents?

**Page 88**

**B. Tense Contrast**  Listen to these sentences. Decide the tense of the verb. Circle *present, past,* or *future.*

1. Hoang needs money for college.
2. He works at Video World.
3. Hoang and Steve became friends.
4. Do you have seventy-five cents?
5. I'll pay you back.
6. Steve never paid him back.
7. Steve forgot his wallet.
8. Hoang never saw his ten dollars again.
9. Steve needs a haircut.
10. Hoang isn't going to lend Steve any more money.

## PRONUNCIATION

**Page 89**

**A. To**  Listen to these common reductions for *to.* Then complete the sentences.

**Examples:**
want to – wanna
need to – needta *or* needa
going to – gonna
have to – hafta
has to – hasta

1. I need to get a haircut.
2. I have to buy some gas.
3. He has to earn money for college.
4. I need to work part time.
5. I want to get a soda.
6. I have to make a phone call.
7. He has to pay for his clothes.
8. I'm going to borrow some money.
9. I want to take a break.
10. He's going to pay the bill.

**Page 89**

**B. Linking Sounds (consonant – vowel)**  Listen carefully and complete these sentences. Mark the linking sounds.

> When a final consonant is followed by a vowel, the sounds are linked. The final consonant sounds like part of the next word.
>  He works on Saturday.

1. Hoang is a college student.
2. He needed a part-time job.
3. He needed money for his books and clothes.
4. He found a job at Video World.
5. He works in the evenings.
6. He works on the weekends.
7. Hoang is friendly with all the workers.
8. I'd like a soda.
9. He never saw his ten dollars again.
10. I need a haircut.

## CONVERSATIONS

**Page 90**

### Conversation 1

A: Dave, can I borrow a quarter? I need to make a phone call.
B: Here. Is that all you need?
A: Yeah. Thanks.

### Conversation 2

A: Sue, could you lend me your car? Just for an hour?
B: Pete, it isn't my car. It's my parents.
A: I just need to mail this package at the post office.
B: Sorry, Pete. I can't lend it to anyone. My parents would shoot me!

### Conversation 3

A: Look at this great sweater. I love the color. Hmm, it's only thirty-five dollars. I have twenty. Can I borrow fifteen? I'll pay you back tomorrow.
B: Sure, no problem.

### Conversation 4

A: Gee, that's a great CD you have, Liz. Could I borrow it to make a tape?

B: Well, remember last week you borrowed that other CD?
A: Yeah.
B: Well, you never gave it back.
A: I . . . I . . . didn't return it?
B: Nope.
A: Look, I'll check and see if I have it and I'll give it to you tomorrow.
B: OK. And when I have it, I'll lend you this one.

### Conversation 5

A: Dan, can I borrow your lawn mower again this week? Ours is still in the repair shop.
B: Well, you know, last week it was empty after you used it. I had to go out and get more gas for it.
A: Oh, gee, I'm really sorry. I forgot to get gas. Don't worry, after I use it this time, it'll be full.
B: I'm using it this morning. You can have it this afternoon.

### Conversation 6

A: Larry, I lost my math book.  I don't know what happened to it. Can I borrow your book tonight to do my homework?
B: Well, I need it to do my homework, too.
A: Ummm, when are you going to do your homework?
B: I guess some time this afternoon.
A: Well, do you think I could work with you and we could do the homework at the same time?
B: That's fine. You want to meet in the library at 3:00?
A: Yeah, OK.

**Page 90**

**B. Meaning**  Listen to each sentence. Circle the letter of the sentence with the same meaning.

1. Is that all you need?
2. Just for an hour?
3. My parents would shoot me.
4. You never gave it back.
5. It was empty after you used it.
6. After I use it this time, it'll be full.

**Page 91**

**C. Yes / No / Maybe**  One speaker is asking to borrow something. Decide if the second person is saying *yes*, *no*, or *maybe*. Circle *Yes*, *No*, or *Maybe*.

1. A: Can I borrow your tennis racquet?
   B: Any time.
2. A: Can I borrow ten dollars?
   B: Sorry, I'm broke.
3. A: Could you lend me your large coffee pot? I'm having a family party.
   B: Of course.
4. A: Can I borrow your long blue dress?
   B: My new one? Oh, I'm not sure.
5. A: Could you lend me that tape?
   B: I'd like to, but it's not mine.

6. A: Can I use your dictionary?
   B: Sure.
7. A: Can I borrow your science notebook tonight?
   B: I don't know. It has all my important notes in it.

# UNIT 12: The World Trade Center

## COMPREHENSION

### Page 95

### Story

On February 26, 1993, a giant explosion shook the World Trade Center. One minute later, smoke began to fill the stairways, halls, and offices. All power and emergency systems were knocked out. There were no lights, no elevators, and no electricity. Over fifty thousand people were working in the building at the time.

It was 12:18 on a typical work day. People were making business calls, writing reports, or attending business meetings. Many were on their lunch break and were eating in one of the building's cafeterias. Also, thousands of people were visiting the building. Some were standing on the observation floor, others were eating lunch at Windows on the World, an expensive restaurant on the top floor.

The bomb exploded in the basement area. One woman was getting out of her car in the parking garage; it blew off her shoes. A man was waiting for the train; it blew off his hat. A secretary was typing at her desk. She fell through the floor sitting in her chair.

In the building, people were not sure what to do. Smoke was coming up the stairs and into the offices. Was the building on fire? Should they stay in their offices? Should they start to walk down the stairs?

Most people decided to walk. There were no lights on the stairways and people were falling and tripping. Everyone was coughing because of the heavy smoke. But most people were calm. Some people counted steps, some people sang. Over sixty thousand workers and visitors walked down the stairs that day, some from the 80th, 90th, and 100th floors. For people on the top floors, the walk down took two or more hours. As people left the building, emergency workers were waiting with oxygen, warm drinks, and blankets.

Some people said they would never go back into the building. They said, "I just can't go back up there. Not now, not ever." But others were ready to go back to work again soon. They said, "It happened. It's over."

### Page 96

### E. Comprehension Questions   Listen and circle the correct answer.

1. Did the workers know what was happening?
2. When did the explosion occur?
3. Where was the most dangerous place to be when the bomb exploded?
4. What was the most serious problem?
5. How did people on the 80th floor get out of the building?
6. How did some people stay calm?
7. Will all the workers return to this building?

## STRUCTURE

### Page 96

### A. Past Continuous Tense   Listen to these sentences. Write the past continuous verb you hear.

1. Over fifty thousand people were working in the building.
2. People were making business calls.
3. Other people were writing reports.
4. Some people were eating in the cafeterias.
5. Thousands of people were visiting the building.
6. Some people were standing on the observation deck.
7. One man was waiting for the train.
8. A secretary was typing at her desk.
9. People were falling.
10. Everyone was coughing from the smoke.

## PRONUNCIATION

### Page 97

### A. Negative Contractions   Listen and complete these sentences with the negative contraction.

> In a negative contraction, we often do not hear the final **t**.
>
> | were | — | weren'**t** | is | — | isn'**t** |
> | was | — | wasn'**t** | did | — | didn'**t** |
> | could | — | couldn'**t** | | | |

1. The power wasn't working.
2. There weren't any lights on the stairways.
3. She wasn't sure what to do.
4. People didn't know what to do.
5. The elevators didn't work.
6. People couldn't get out of the elevators.
7. There weren't any flames.
8. People didn't panic; they stayed calm.
9. He isn't going back into the building.
10. Some workers won't return to work.

### Page 97

### B. Linking Sounds (consonant – vowel)   Listen carefully and complete these sentences. Mark the linking sounds.

> When a final consonant is followed by a vowel, the sounds are linked. The final consonant sounds like part of the next word.
> Emergency workers were waiting **with oxygen.**

1. Smoke began to fill the halls and offices.
2. All power was knocked out.
3. Many people were on their lunch break.

4. Some people were eating lunch at Windows on the World.
5. The bomb exploded in the basement area.
6. One woman was in the basement.
7. The bomb blew off her shoes.
8. There were no lights on the stairways.
9. I will never go back up there.
10. It's over.

## CONVERSATIONS

**Page 98**

### Conversation 1

A: Have you ever seen a fire?
B: You mean in a house?
A: Yeah, in a house, a car . . . anywhere.
B: No.
A: No?
B: No. I've seen the remains, but, the actual fire . . . No. I haven't seen that. I've driven by and seen smoke when it was all over.
A: When it was all over?
B: Well, one day when we were driving up the parkway, the police were there and there was a car on the side and there was a lot of smoke and the fire engines were there but they had put the fire out already. This poor man was standing by the side. He looked so upset. But I didn't actually see the flames or the firefighters putting it out.

### Conversation 2

A: Did you ever see a fire?
B: A fire? Like a big fire?
A: Well, a big one. A little one. Either.
B: Well, we had a small one in my house. One night, we ordered pizza, two big ones. And there was some pizza left. My mom asked my brother to put the food away and he put one of the pizzas in the box in the oven 'cause it was too big to put in the refrigerator. But my mom didn't know that he put it there. The next night, my mom turned on the oven. And in about five minutes, these flames started to come out of the oven. My mom opened the oven with a towel and grabbed the pizza box and threw it on the floor. Then she threw water on it. There's still, like, this small black spot on our floor. Boy, my mom was so mad at my brother.

### Conversation 3

A: Did you ever see a fire?
B: Yes, about 20 years ago. A terrible fire.
A: What happened?
B: Well, it was night. There were lots of flames. There was a big crowd of people watching. The firefighters were rescuing people. Well, you know, they were taking people out of the building.
A: They were taking them out?
B: You know, with ladders. They were carrying them down.
A: Where was this? Somebody's house?

B: No, it was an old apartment building. A real big one . . . for senior citizens. Maybe sixty, seventy people lived there.
A: Was everybody all right?
B: No, I think a few people died.

### Conversation 4

A: You had a fire at your house a couple of years ago, didn't you?
B: Oh, yes. I wasn't there. But, yes, we did.
A: What happened?
B: Well, there was some Chinese food in the refrigerator, from one of those take-out places. And it was in one of those little boxes; you know, the kind with the metal handles. And my daughter wanted to heat it up, so she put it in the microwave. And it started smoking inside, a lot. And she started to panic. I think all she needed to do was open the door. But she didn't do that. She went running for her father. And all the time it continued to smoke. He came into the kitchen and unplugged the microwave. But it kept on smoking. Finally, it stopped. It destroyed the microwave.

**Page 99**

**C. And / But**  When telling a story in English, speakers frequently use *and* or *but* to connect ideas and to continue the conversation. Listen to these sentences. If you hear *and* or *but*, circle it. If you hear no connecting word, circle *c*.

1. The police were there and there was a car on the side.
2. This poor man was standing by the side. He looked upset.
3. One night we ordered pizza, two big ones and there was a little left.
4. Then he put the box of pizza in the oven but my mom didn't know he put it there.
5. The next night my mom turned on the stove. And in about five minutes, these flames started to come out of the oven.
6. These flames started to come out of the oven. My mom opened the oven door with a towel.
7. There were a lot of flames. There was a big crowd of people watching.
8. The food was in one of those little boxes. And my daughter wanted to heat it up.
9. It started smoking a lot. And she started to panic.
10. All she needed to do was open the door. But she didn't do that.

# UNIT 13: The Titanic

## COMPREHENSION

**Page 103**

### Story

Millionaire Arthur Ryerson stepped on board the Titanic, the world's most famous luxury ship. He was going to enjoy this trip across the Atlantic. This was the

Titanic's first voyage, a trip from England to New York City. Her decks were filled with libraries, smoking rooms, dining rooms, a gymnasium, and a swimming pool.

When the Titanic pulled out of port on April 10, 1912, she was carrying 2,224 passengers and crew. The first four days of the trip were clear, calm, and cold. Arthur Ryerson spent his days talking, walking, and playing cards with several of his friends. All the passengers were enjoying their days aboard the ship. None of them knew of the danger ahead. They were approaching icebergs.

The evening of April 14 was relaxed and friendly. By 11:30, most passengers were sleeping or getting ready for bed. Other passengers were reading, drinking, or writing letters. The band was finishing for the evening. Arthur Ryerson was playing cards with three of his friends.

Out in the cold, one of the crewmen was standing watch. Suddenly, up ahead, he saw something in the water. He immediately rang three bells and radioed the engine room. "Iceberg, right ahead! Stop!" It was too late. The iceberg ripped a 300-foot hole in the Titanic's right side. The ship was filling with water and sinking fast.

There was no panic on board. Arthur Ryerson was one of the men who helped women and children into the lifeboats. When he saw there would be no room for himself or any of the other men on the ship, Ryerson and his three friends returned to the smoking room and their game of cards. They were still playing as the Titanic sank into the icy waters. On that cold evening in 1912, 1,513 people lost their lives in one of the worst sea disasters in history.

**Page 104**

**E. Listen and Answer**   Listen to these questions about what people were doing on the night of April 14. Write the number of the question in front of the correct answer.

1. What was Arthur Ryerson doing when the ship hit the iceberg?
2. What were most of the passengers doing when the ship hit the iceberg?
3. What was the band doing when they heard the alarm?
4. What was the crew doing as the ship was sinking?
5. What was the radioman doing as the ship was sinking?
6. What were the women and children doing when the ship sank?
7. What was Arthur Ryerson doing when the ship sank?

**Page 104**

**F. Comprehension Questions**   Listen and circle the correct answer.

1. Where was the ship traveling?
2. In which part of the Atlantic Ocean did the ship hit the iceberg?
3. What was the weather at the time of the accident?
4. Who saw the iceberg first?
5. Who got into the lifeboats first?
6. What did Athur Ryerson do after the ship hit the iceberg?
7. Why did so many people lose their lives?

**STRUCTURE**

**Page 105**

**A. Past Continuous Tense**   Listen to these sentences. Write the past continuous verb you hear.

1. The Titanic was carrying 2,224 passengers and crew.
2. All the passengers were enjoying their days aboard the ship.
3. They were approaching icebergs.
4. Most passengers were sleeping.
5. Others were getting ready for bed.
6. The band was finishing for the evening.
7. Arthur Ryerson was playing cards.
8. One of the crewmen was standing watch.
9. The ship was filling with water.
10. It was sinking fast.

**PRONUNCIATION**

**Page 105**

**A. Of**   Listen carefully and complete these sentences with *of* and the missing words.

> We often do not hear the **f** in the word of.
> Before a vowel or an **h, f** sounds like **v**.
>
> the decks o͜f the ship
>
> ov͜ April
>
> ov͜ his friends

1. The Titanic pulled out of port on April 10, 1912.
2. The first four days of the trip were clear and cold.
3. Arthur Ryerson was playing cards with several of his friends.
4. None of them knew of the danger ahead.
5. The evening of April 14 was relaxed.
6. He was in a smoking room with three of his friends.
7. One of the crewmen was standing watch.
8. There was no room for any of the men.
9. He returned to his game of cards.
10. It was one of the worst sea disasters in history.

**Page 106**

**B. Word Stress**   Listen carefully and mark the stressed words.

> The most important words in a sentence are stressed. They are longer and louder. These are the content words (nouns, verbs, adjectives, and adverbs).
>
> It was a **cóld níght.**

1. The Titanic was a luxury ship.
2. It was traveling from England to New York.
3. It was clear and cold.
4. The ship was approaching icebergs.
5. A crewman was standing watch.
6. He saw something in the water.

7. The ship hit an iceberg.
8. They radioed for help.
9. There was no panic.
10. The ship sank.

## SPEAKERS

### Page 106

### Speaker 1

We had a tornado watch system. There were always people who were on tornado watch. And when anybody saw one, they'd call and the town would blow this siren. And we were supposed to go into the basement. Most of the time, we just saw tornados in the distance. But they got close enough once or twice that we all ran inside and down into the basement. One time, one hit the next town and my dad drove us over there the next day. It did terrible damage. The tornado hit two of the houses on this one street and they just exploded. That was the end of those houses. There were no walls and no roof. Just some wood and a couple of pieces of furniture lying around.

### Speaker 2

We live on a hillside. We worry about mud slides. And there's a hill in our backyard. A big hill. It goes up 50 or 60 feet. Almost straight up. The back of our house, it's all windows and glass. Our bedroom is all windows and we have a big sliding glass door in the living room. And I keep thinking, someday, that hill is going to be in our bedroom with us. Usually, it's really dry out here and nobody worries. But this past spring, it rained so much, people around us began to get worried.

### Speaker 3

We have earthquake drills at school. When a special bell goes off, we have *duck and cover*. That means we get under our desks. We have big heavy desks, and we get under them and put our heads between our knees. And we put our arms over our necks and heads. Then on the second bell we evacuate to the football field. After the earthquake there are sometimes aftershocks, you know, some more smaller earthquakes, and they want us outside so that nothing can fall on us.

### Speaker 4

I lived in the middle of New York State and we're not supposed to have hurricanes there. But we had one when I was about 12. I remember watching the trees coming down. I never saw trees moving like that before. I mean, huge trees coming down. They got pulled out of the ground from their roots. That was pretty scary. Around us, so many trees came down. On my street, about ten trees were down in the street. We didn't have electricity or telephone service. No emergency vehicles could pass, no police or fire engines. No one could get to work. School was closed all week.

### Page 107

**B. Listen and Decide** Listen and circle the letter of the idea that follows.

1. We had a tornado watch system.
2. When anybody saw a tornado, they'd call.
3. The tornado hit two houses on one street.
4. That was the end of those houses.
5. We live on a hillside.
6. This past spring it rained a lot.
7. When a special bell goes off, we have *duck and cover*.
8. After the earthquake there are sometimes aftershocks.
9. I lived in the middle of New York State.
10. I never saw trees moving like that before.

### Page 107

**C. Past or Present** Decide if the speaker is talking about a present situation or is describing an event that happened in the past. Circle *present* or *past*.

1. We had a tornado watch system.
2. We have earthquake drills at school.
3. It's really so dry out here that no one worries about mud slides.
4. It rained so much that everyone began to worry about mud slides.
5. I never saw trees moving like that before.
6. There's never any warning for an earthquake.
7. After an earthquake there are sometimes aftershocks; you know, some smaller earthquakes.
8. No one could get to work.

## UNIT 14: Recycling

### COMPREHENSION

### Page 111

### Story

Some people say that the United States is a throwaway society. Everything we don't want, we just throw away in the garbage — newspapers, soda cans, disposable diapers, shampoo bottles.

Most of the garbage in the United States is buried in areas called landfills. Garbage trucks empty trash into the landfills, then tractors crush it and cover it with dirt. But, many cities and towns have no more room in their landfills.

A few years ago, three thousand tons of garbage from Islip, Long Island, became famous. The garbage was on a long flat boat. The boat sailed to North Carolina, but officials there said, "No, thanks. We decided that we don't want your garbage." The boat went to Florida, then to Louisiana. The same thing happened. The captain tried to pay Mexico to take the garbage, but they didn't want it, either. After six months, the boat returned again to Long Island. New York City agreed to burn the garbage. Islip agreed to take the ashes. This news story woke people up. They began to ask, "What are we going to do with all our garbage?"

Recycling is one answer. Some cities require people to separate used cans, bottles, plastic, and newspapers. Special collection trucks pick up the materials from in front of homes or people take the materials to recycling centers. From there, it goes to different factories. Some factories make new aluminum cans from old ones or new glass bottles from old ones. Some factories use old newspapers to make paper and cardboard boxes. Other factories manufacture flower pots and park benches and carpets from old plastic.

Recycling saves trees, metal, and other natural resources. It also saves energy. When you buy a product, look for the recycling symbol. It means that the product was made from recycled material. By recycling and buying recycled products, we can all do a part to save the environment.

**Page 112**

**D. Second Listening**   You will hear part of the story again. Put these pictures in order and explain what happened to the garbage from the town of Islip, Long Island.

A few years ago, three thousand tons of garbage from Islip, Long Island, became famous. The garbage was on a long flat boat. The boat sailed to North Carolina, but officials there said, "No, thanks. We decided that we don't want your garbage." The boat went to Florida, then to Louisiana. The same thing happened. The captain tried to pay Mexico to take the garbage, but they didn't want it, either. After six months, the boat returned again to Long Island. New York City agreed to burn the garbage. Islip agreed to take the ashes. This news story woke people up. They began to ask, "What are we going to do with all our garbage?"

**Page 112**

**E. Recycling**   You will hear part of the story again. Write one use for each of these recycled products.

Recycling is one answer. Some cities require people to separate used cans, bottles, plastic, and newspapers. Special collection trucks pick up the materials from in front of homes or people take the materials to recycling centers. From there, it goes to different factories. Some factories make new aluminum cans from old ones or new glass bottles from old ones. Some factories use old newspapers to make paper and cardboard boxes. Other factories manufacture flower pots and park benches and carpets from old plastic.

**Page 113**

**F. Comprehension Questions**   Listen and circle the correct answer.

1. What does a throwaway society produce?
2. What's done with most of the garbage in the United States?
3. Why did the garbage from Islip become famous?
4. What did people learn from the Islip, Long Island, news story?
5. Why is it necessary to separate materials for recycling?
6. Why should people recycle?
7. How do people know if a product can be recycled?

## STRUCTURE
**Page 113**

**A. Tense Contrast**   Listen to these sentences. Write the verb you hear.

1. Garbage trucks empty trash into the landfills.
2. Towns have no more room in their landfills.
3. The boat sailed to North Carolina.
4. The same thing happened.
5. The boat returned to Long Island.
6. What are we going to do with all our garbage?
7. This story woke people up.
8. Special trucks pick up the materials.
9. Recycling saves trees.
10. We can all help.

## PRONUNCIATION
**Page 114**

**A. Linking Sounds (Same Consonant)**   Listen carefully and complete these sentences with the linked words. Mark the linking sounds.

> At times, the same sound or a similar sound is at the end of one word and at the beginning of the next word. The words are linked. We use the same sound for both words.
>   The boat turned back to New York.

1. There was no more room in the landfill.
2. The officials said, "No, thanks."
3. The captain tried to pay Mexico.
4. The boat went to Florida.
5. New York City agreed to burn the garbage.
6. This news story woke people up.
7. Most towns require recycling.
8. We can all do a part to save the environment.

**Page 114**

**B. Word Stress**   Listen carefully to these questions and answers. Mark the stressed word(s) in the answer.

> We often stress the answer to a question, especially if the answer is in contrast to the question.
>   Can I recycle window glass?
>   No, you can only recycle **bottles** and **jars**.

1. A: Do you have a recycling center?
   B: No, we have curbside pickup.
2. A: Does the truck come every week?
   B: No, it comes every other week.
3. A: Does it come on Thursday?
   B: No, it comes on Monday.
4. A: Do you pay for this service?
   B: No, it's free.
5. A: Do you recycle a lot of cans?
   B: No, I recycle a lot of bottles.
6. A: Do you have curbside pickup?
   B: No, we have a recycling center.
7. A: Is it near your house?
   B: No, it's ten miles from here.
8. A: Can you recycle food boxes?
   B: No, but we can recycle cardboard boxes.
9. A: Do you have to separate tin cans and aluminum cans?
   B: No, we can put them in the same container.
10. A: Can you bring leaves to the recycling center?
    B: No, we have to bring them to the conservation center.

## SPEAKERS

**Page 115**

### Speaker 1

There's a big garbage dump about two or three miles from our town. And the garbage trucks and people take all their garbage there. Well, they don't do anything, like they don't cover it with dirt. In the summer, it smells so bad, we can smell it in town sometimes.

### Speaker 2

Garbage is a big problem in my country. People put their garbage in bags and put it outside. But we never know when the sanitation people are coming. Sometimes it's once a week. Sometimes they wait ten days. So the garbage is like a mountain. It's OK in the winter but it smells terrible in the summer.

### Speaker 3

We keep our garbage inside. If we take it outside, all the dogs in the neighborhood go through it. When the garbage truck comes, the driver rings a bell. And the people come out of their houses with their baskets, and bags and the garbage truck takes everything away.

### Speaker 4

We don't recycle in my country. We throw everything in the garbage: bottles, cans, plastic. We throw it all out together.

### Speaker 5

In my country, the stores don't give you brown paper bags or plastic bags, even at the supermarket. If you want bags, you buy them. So everybody uses their brown bags again and again or they have cloth bags.

### Speaker 6

In the United States, people only go to the supermarket once or twice a week and they buy a lot of food. But in my country, we go to the store every day, maybe one store for bread, one for meat, and another for fruit and vegetables. We don't have big packages and boxes for everything. Like for meat, the store owner just wraps it in a piece of paper.

**Page 116**

**C. Agree or Disagree** Listen to these statements about recycling. Compare them with recycling in your country. After you hear the statement, check one of the statements to show the situation in your country.

1. We recycle everything.
2. We have to pay for paper bags.
3. We pay for garbage disposal.
4. Sometimes the store gives you a bag, sometimes it doesn't.
5. We burn our garbage.
6. We have open landfills.
7. We never know when the garbage truck is coming.
8. We can throw anything into the garbage.

# UNIT 15: Dreams

## COMPREHENSION

**Page 121**

### Story

Did you dream last night? What did you dream about? You might not remember your dreams, but people usually dream four to six times a night. Dreams can be short, only about ten minutes, or can continue for an hour or more. People dream in color.

At times, we all remember a dream. In our dreams, we might take a trip or look back at our childhood. We might run away from a tiger or see a terrible accident. Someone we love might die.

What is the meaning of these dreams? Many psychologists believe that dreams are "night work." They help us look at situations and fears in our daily lives. In our dreams, we face problems and try to solve them. We look at our fears. We try out different personalities; at times we might be aggressive and talkative and at other times we might be frightened and shy.

We often dream in symbols. Symbols are pictures that stand for or mean something else. A king and a queen might represent our parents. Small animals might stand for children. A long journey might mean we are worried about death or the death of someone in our family. If we are crossing a river, it might mean that we are at an important decision or time in our lives. If we get across the river in the dream, we believe we will be successful. If we do not make it across, we are afraid of failure.

We can have the same dream over and over. The dream may always be the same or it might have different endings. Our minds are working and playing, making movies about our lives.

**Page 122**

**D. Second Listening**   Listen to these statements. Circle *T* if the statement is true, *F* if the statement is false.

1. People have only one or two dreams a week.
2. People forget most of their dreams.
3. A typical dream is a few seconds or minutes long.
4. Dreams are in black and white.
5. In a dream, a person might act very differently than in real life.
6. In a dream, a person might try to find a solution to a problem.
7. It's possible to have the same dream many times.
8. Dreams tell people what the future will bring.

## STRUCTURE

**Page 123**

**A. Might**   Listen to these sentences. Write the complete verb you hear.

1. You might see a terrible accident in your dream.
2. You might look back at your childhood.
3. You might run away from a tiger.
4. A dream might continue for an hour.
5. A king and queen might represent your parents.
6. Small animals might stand for children.
7. Someone we love might die.
8. We might take a trip.
9. You might not remember your dreams.
10. You might have the same dream again and again.

## PRONUNCIATION

**Page 123**

**A. Word Stress**   Listen carefully and mark the stressed word in each pair.

> Stress can put special emphasis on any word in a sentence. Stress can change the meaning of the sentence.
> I **néver** dream.
> **Í** never dream.

1. a. He **snores** all night.
   b. He snores **all night.**
2. a. You **should** go to bed earlier.
   b. You should go to bed **earlier.**
3. a. I **want** to hear about your dream.
   b. I want to hear about **your** dream.
4. a. What's the **meaning** of that dream?
   b. What's the meaning of **that** dream?

5. a. Dreams can be **frightening.**
   b. Dreams **can** be frightening.
6. a. I can't tell **her** my dream.
   b. I **can't** tell her my dream.
7. a. I **never** have nightmares.
   b. **I** never have nightmares.

**Page 124**

**B. Do / Did**   Listen to these questions about sleep and dreams. Circle the first two words of each question, *Do you* or *Did you.*

> *Did you* often sounds like *Didja.*
>   Didja dream last night?
> *Do you* often sounds like *Dya.*
>   Dya dream a lot?

1. Do you dream a lot?
2. Did you dream last night?
3. Do you remember your dreams?
4. Do you dream in color?
5. Did you ever have a nightmare?
6. Did you ever walk in your sleep?
7. Do you sometimes talk in your sleep?
8. Did you ever dream about your parents?
9. Did you ever dream about your job?
10. Do you speak in English in your dreams?

## DREAMS

**Page 124**

### Dream 1

I had a terrible dream last night. It was about my father. I saw him very clearly. He was on a ladder, very high, washing windows. It was the house where we used to live when I was a child. And I called, "Dad, be careful." Because he wasn't holding on. And he smiled and said, "Don't worry." Then he started to fall, very, very slowly. It seemed that he was falling for two or three minutes, in slow motion. And I tried to scream, but I couldn't. And he hit the ground.

### Dream 2

I sometimes dream that I'm pregnant or that someone leaves a baby at our front door. You know, I already have three children and I don't want any more, so I don't know why I dream this.

### Dream 3

When I was younger, I had, oh boy, these dreams, mostly about my parents, often about my mother. And I sometimes redream my dreams, I dream them again and again until I dream them right. And I remember this one dream especially.

My mother and her friends and I were leaving the supermarket. We were walking into the parking lot. And as we were getting in the car, this group of men came up and stood all around us. They were no good. Now, I tried to get everybody in the car, but I couldn't get everybody in the car. And I woke up and it was like, BOOM! Wrong! And I went back to sleep again and I redreamed it. This time, I got everybody in the car, and I closed the door, but the window was open. This man was able to get his hand in. I woke up and I said, "Uh-uh. Oh no." I went back to sleep again. And this last time in my dream, I got everybody in, got the door closed, the window closed, and drove off.

### Dream 4

A few nights ago, I had a dream that something was chasing me. I don't remember how the dream began, but I was running. I was running through the woods. Well, it was more like a jungle, the trees and grass and bushes were really thick. I was running and screaming. Some kind of animal was behind me, I couldn't see it, but I heard it. It made a lot of noise, like a pig. Then my husband woke me up and said, "What's the matter? You're crying. It's all right. You're having a nightmare."

### Dream 5

At times I dream about finding money. It's never a lot of money, it's always coins. I'm walking down the street. And I look on the sidewalk and I see a few quarters and dimes. I walk a little further, and there's another five or six quarters. Then I look ahead, and I see money, but just coins, everywhere, on the sidewalk and on the street and under the cars. I just pick them up and put them in my pockets.

### Dream 6

I have a recurring dream about a river. I'm young, about 11 or 12. I'm playing by the river with my brother and sister. It's a big, wide river. And suddenly, in the middle, we see a young woman in the river. She's holding on to something, I think it's a piece of wood. She's calling for help. There's no adult around and no boat and we don't know what to do. The river is moving fast, and she moves past us, still calling for help. And we just stand there and watch her going down the river.